Copyright © 2016, 2019 Charles Falkner

All rights reserved. No part of this publication may be reproduced, distributed, or transmitted in any form or by any means, including photocopying, recording, or other electronic or mechanical methods, without the prior written permission of the publisher, except in the case of brief quotations embodied in critical reviews and certain other noncommercial uses permitted by copyright law. For permission requests, write to the publisher, addressed "Attention: Permissions Coordinator," at the address below.

Zeta Publishing, Inc
3850 SE 58th Ave
Ocala, FL 34480
www.zetapublishing.com

The views expressed in this work are solely those of the author and do not necessarily reflect the views of the publisher, and the publisher hereby disclaims any responsibility for them.

Ordering Information:
Quantity sales. Special discounts are available on quantity purchases by corporations, associations, and others. For details, contact the publisher at the address above.
Orders by U.S. trade bookstores and wholesalers. Please contact Zeta Publishing: Tel: (352) 694-2553; Fax: (352) 694-1791 or visit www.zetapublishing.com

First published by Xlibris in 2016

Rev. Date: May 2019

ISBN: 978-1-7335084-0-7 (sc)
ISBN: 978-1-7335084-1-4 (e)

Library of Congress: 2018967506
Printed in the United States of America

Ocala, FL

The Coming Seismic Eruption of Christendom

C. Y. Falkner

Chapter 1

One Way the Whole World Has been Deceived: Revelation 12:9

One way is the use of the word "begotten." The *Strong's Concordance* reference number for the word begotten is 1080 and gives this definition: "to procreate (prop. Of the Father, but by extens, of the Mother); fig. To regenerate: bear, beget, be born, bring forth, conceive; be delivered of, gender, make, spring.",[1] Now, with the meaning of the word in mind, let us see some of the uses of "begotten."

I know you have heard the term "born again." In John 3:3, Jesus said, "I say to you, if one does not receive birth from above, he is not able to see the Kingdom of God.",[2] These are those who have a new life in Christ, and the word "birth" (*Strong's* cross-reference number here is 1080) seems to mean "to regenerate." According to Acts 13:33–34, "That this God has fulfilled to us, their children, raising up Jesus; as also it has been written in the second Psalm 'You are my son; today I have begotten you and that he raised him from the dead; no more being about to return to corruption.'",[3] The word "begotten" is reference number 1080 in *Strong's Concordance* and "be delivered of",[4] because Jesus was delivered from death. Matthew 1:1 mentions,[5] "The Book of the generation of Jesus Christ, the son of Abraham. Abraham fathered Isaac and so on through the lineage. The word "fathered" is in *Strong's* reference number 1080, and this is the prime meaning of "begotten"; the father gave life to the egg of the mother.,[6]

And now we look at the scripture that everyone thinks they know. John 3:16 says, "For God so loved the world he gave his only begotten son, that everyone believing into him should not perish, but have everlasting life."[7] What is wrong is the translation of "only begotten." "Only begotten" is not found here. What should be in the translation of the Bible is "only born." In the Greek Scriptures, that is what it says, and a couple of translations do say "only son" or "only born." James Moffatt's translation does,[8] but no one seems to be aware of it. "Only born" is referenced in *Strong's Concordance* number 3439, and it means "only born or sole."[9]

Now you can see why the church started using "only begotten" to describe Jesus as the son of God. You see they were adopting the belief in the Trinity. In 325 AD, at the Counsel of Nicene, they adopted a creed which said the Father and Son were the same. In 381 AD at Constantinople, they added the word "Spirit" to Father and Son, making it a Trinity. Here is part of the creed: "the only begotten Son of God, begotten from the Father before all ages; light from light, true God from true God, begotten, not made (homoousios) with the Father, through whom all things came into existence."[10] They did not quote from the Bible because it is not there. In later Bible translations into English, "the only begotten" replaced "only born" when referring to Jesus. But in Luke 7:12, it is rendered correctly, saying, "And as he drew near to the Gate of the City, even, behold one having died was being borne, an only son born to his mother, and she was a widow, and a considerable crowd of the City was with her."[11] The reason the church used the term "only begotten" as you now know is because it allows for the son of God to not have a beginning. If John 3:16 is quoted correctly using "only born," then the son had a beginning. The great God's title became Father after the birth of his "only born" son.

The Bible also says that Jesus is the "first born" in Colossians 1:15: "Who is the image of the invisible God, the first born of all creation."[12] Here is what we draw from these facts: Before time began, God existed alone in space. Everything was in this God. The first thing he did was give birth to his "only born" called the Word. Revelation 3:14 says, "And to the angel of the Church of Laodicea, write: these things says the Amen, the faithful and true witness, the beginning of the Creation of God."[13] There are other beginnings mentioned, such as that in John 1:1, and while they say "the" in front of those beginnings, it is not there in the original writings except in Revelation 3:14. John 1:14 says, "And the word became flesh, and tabernacled among us, and we behold his glory, glory as an 'only born' from the Father, full of grace and of truth."[14] So there are many beginnings, but only one "The Beginning" which was when the Father gave birth to the Word of God. The Word who later became Jesus had a beginning.

So now you can see that the Trinity is a false teaching that started around 325 AD and became full blown at around 800 AD.

Another religious teaching is that Jesus's life started when Mary gave birth to him, and all things the Bible seems to say regarding his prehuman existence was all like a dream in God's mind. Luke 1:35 says, "The Holy Spirit will come on you, and the power of the most High will over Shadow you—for this reason also that Holy One being born of you will be called Son of God."[15] Now we already know that God gave birth to his "only born" and became his "only born son" when Mary gave him a body of flesh. For Jesus to be an "only born" of Mary, he would have been her only child, and Matthew 12:47 says, "Then one said to him, behold, your mother and your "brothers" are standing outside, seeking to speak to you."[16]

So God gave birth to the "only born" Word of God. God became a Father. The Word became flesh through Mary and became the "only born son" of God who purchased the whole world of mankind.

Thus, that religious teaching is just another way the world of mankind is being deceived.

Chapter 2

Who Is Christ?

Matthew 24:24 reads: "For false Christs will rise up, and they will give great signs and wonders, so as to lead astray, if possible even the Elect."[1]

Revelation 12:9 reads: "Satan has deceived the habitable world."[2] Read Matthew 24:24 again as it is saying there are many false christs and prophets, and they mislead the habitable world, and they try to mislead even the Elect. The false Christ takes the place of the Christ, and the Antichrist is in place of the Christ.

1 John 2:18 reads: "Young ones, it is the last hour, and as you heard that the antichrist is coming, even now many antichrist have risen up, from which you know that it is the last hour."[3] The last hour is the last hour for the church. But the reason for reading it is to show that the false christs and Antichrist are the same; both are in place of the Christ. So here's the problem: there are many false christs and Antichrists and many religions, all with their versions of who the Christ is, and the Bible says the habitable world has been misled. We want to follow *the Christ*. The purpose of this study is to help us to identify *the Christ*.

Here are a few beliefs that reflect on the versions of many religions. *Hell*—most religions teach it as a place of torment. *Strong's Concordance* in the Hebrew (cross-reference number 7585) and in the Greek language (cross-reference number 86) both say "the world of the dead"[4] and "grave," "hell," and "pit." All religions have their set of doctrines that make their religions what they are, and if their doctrines are proven to be false, that religion is destroyed, so you can see why all these wars and burnings of individuals took place. One example is that of Servetus in the sixteenth century. He was a medical doctor who also studied theology. He came to believe that infant baptism was wrong, and he came to believe that Jesus did not have a prehuman existence but became God's only begotten son when Mary gave birth to Jesus, meaning that human birth was his beginning. Now if these beliefs were true, they would expose the religion that taught otherwise. That is why John Calvin, in 1553, had Servetus burned to death while saying that Servetus was going to hell and burn forever. You can read about that in page 289 of *A History of Christianity* by Paul Johnson.[5]

Now back to the subject of hell, which also translates to "grave." In the King James Bible, in Psalms 49:15, it reads "But God will redeem my soul from the grave: for he shall receive me." If your Bible has a marginal reference, the word "grave" has a number. Look at that number in the margin and it will say "hell," and in Psalms 55:15, it is the opposite, which proves that the translator knew that hell and the grave are the same.[6] Revelation 20:18 reads "And the sea gave up the dead in it, and death and Hades gave up the dead in them, and they were each judged according to their works."[7] "Hades" is the Greek word that means "grave" or "hell," which proves that people who are in hell or the grave are dead.

Another word that most religions point to in support of tormenting people forever is the Greek "Gehenna," mostly translated as "hellfire," and *Strong's* cross-reference number 1067 says "valley of (the son of) Hinnem." Gehenna was a valley that Jesus used figuratively as a name for the place (or state) of everlasting punishment.[8] That valley was outside the wall of Jerusalem, and that is where the city dumped garbage, dead animals, and bodies of dead criminals. They used burning sulfur to destroy whatever was thrown in, and there were worms around the edges of the sulfur and fire so that what was not consumed by the fire was consumed by the worms, as mentioned in Mark 9:48, which pictures complete destruction,[9] or as Revelation 20:14 reads, "And death and Hades were thrown into the lake of fire. This is the second death."[10]

The first death was the death caused by our father Adam who sinned against God and passed it on to all of us. Jesus purchased us from that death. John 3:16 says, "For God so loved the world that he gave his only born son, that everyone believing in him should have everlasting life."[11] The second death is when one knows God's Word and his son and speaks against it. Hebrews 10:26 says, "For if we are willfully sinning after receiving the full knowledge of the truth, there remains no more sacrifice concerning sins."[12] What this is saying is dying the second time is forever.

The next doctrine is the immortality of the soul. In the *Hebrew Scriptures Strong's Concordance*, cross-reference number 5315 says "a breathing creature."[13] By turning to the Bible, we can understand what it really means.

First, there is not one scripture in the Bible saying the soul is immortal. Most religions have been teaching only man has a soul. Now here are a few scriptures that will help to know what a soul is. In Genesis 1:30, it says, "And to every living thing of the earth, and to every bird of the heavens and to every creeper on the earth, in which is a living soul, every green plant is for food. And it was so."[14]

Genesis 2:19 says, "And Jehovah God formed every animal of the field, and every bird of the heavens out of the ground, and he brought them to the man, to see what he would call it. And all which the man might call it, each living soul, that was its name."[15] As you can see, marine life such as fish, animals on Earth, and birds of heaven are all souls, and they do not have eternal life, and as for man, Ezekiel 18:4 says, "The soul that sins, it itself will die."[16]

Now we know that the soul is mortal. That is why we love God for the scripture in John 3:16: "For God so loved the world that he gave his only born son, that everyone believing into him should not perish, but have everlasting."[17] That is why the ransom was paid so mankind can have eternal life.

Next is the doctrine that when we die, we go to heaven. Let me introduce to you how this belief got its start. Read Genesis 1:28: "And god blessed them; and God said to them, Be Fruitful and multiply, and fill the earth and subdue it and rule over the fish of the sea and over birds of the heavens, and over all living things creeping on the earth."[18] What this says is Adam and Eve were to fill the earth with sons and daughters and subdue or turn the earth into a paradise and take care of all the animals. For this to happen, Jehovah God had a standard that would guide mankind and ensure eternal life for all mankind. In order to teach Adam and Eve this standard, God said in Genesis 2:17, "But of the tree of knowledge of good and evil you may not eat, for in the day that you eat of it, you shall surely die."[19] God gave this information to Adam, and he was to teach this to Eve and all their sons and daughters. Now Adam did teach Eve about this command, but let us see where he missed the mark of righteous. Read Genesis 3:1–6, which says, "And the serpent was cunning above every animal of the field which Jehovah God had made, and he said, is it true that God has said, you shall not eat from any tree of the garden? And the woman said to the serpent, we may eat of the fruit of the trees of the garden, but of the fruit of the tree, which is in the middle of the garden, God has said, you shall not eat of it, nor shall you touch it, lest you die. And the serpent said to the woman, you shall not surely die, for God knows that for the day you eat of it, your eyes shall be opened and you shall be as God, knowing good and evil, and the woman saw that the tree was good for food and that it was pleasant to the eyes, and the tree was desirable to make one wise. She took of its fruit and ate; and she also gave to her husband with her and he ate."[20] As you can see, this is the first lie recorded in the Bible. Satan told Eve you will not die and you can set up your own standard of good and evil. Now as far as setting your standard of good and evil you can do that, but it will bring disappointment and death, just like eating of the fruit of the tree did.

As for eating of the fruit of the tree, let's read 1 Timothy 2:14, where it says, "And Adam was not deceived, but the woman being deceived has to be in transgression: but she will be delivered through the bearing of children, if they remain in faith and love and holiness with sensibleness."[21] What this is saying is that Eve was deceived into violating God's will, but Adam sinned against God and he brought sin and death on all his children or mankind. That is why in Colossians 5:21–22, it says, "For since death is through man also through A man is the resurrection of the dead; for as all die in Adam, so also all will be made alive in Christ."[22] The point is that Eve did not bring death to mankind; it was Adam, and had Adam not eaten of the fruit of the tree, Adam and Eve would have passed on eternal life to all mankind. Some ask, "What about Eve?" Jehovah told Eve and all women to bear children, remain in faith, love, and holiness, and she would be delivered. By the way, that is what she was told when God blessed them at Genesis 1:28 to fill the earth. Here is an interesting bit of information in Genesis 3:22–24: "And Jehovah God said, 'Behold! The man has become as one of us, to know good and evil. And now, lest he put forth his hand and also take from the tree of life and eat and live forever.' And Jehovah God sent him out of the garden of Eden to till the ground out of which he was taken, he drove the man out, and he caused to dwell the cherubs at the east of the garden of Eden, and the flaming sword whirling around, to guard the way of the tree of life."[23] Now as you can see, there were two trees in the garden, and those two trees were to make it possible for mankind to live forever on the earth. The first tree they were to eat of was the tree of knowledge of good and evil, but only after Jehovah God had taught his standards. After they accepted God's standards, then he would lead them to the tree of life, which is why Jehovah God drove man out of the garden of Eden (or paradise) and placed two cherubs with flaming swords to protect the way to the tree of life until they (mankind) knew and accepted God's standard, which is the knowledge of God's good and evil. That is why those doing the laws of God, (you see these laws are drawn from God's standard) will have authority to go to the tree of life. Revelation 22:1–14 shows a picture of the city (New Jerusalem), and in it is Jehovah's throne with the Lamb of God, or Jesus, sitting on the throne with his Father, and from that throne flows a river of pure clear water, and in this city's streets from here to there is a tree of life producing twelve crops a year of fruit, and the leaves are for the healing of nations. That is why in verse 14 it shows that those doing the commands of God are given authority to go to the tree, and they may enter the city. You will notice that those not doing the commands of God cannot enter the city, so they do not get eternal life. But the tree of life was on the earth and will be in the new heavens and Earth. The hope of mankind for life is eternal life on Earth.[24]

Now let us move to 2 Corinthians 5, which most religions believe show souls going to heaven. This chapter is in picturesque language. So if anyone wants to understand the "picture" of this chapter, one has to know his divine purpose. You have to know why he created man and woman, the reason for the Abrahamic Covenant, the reason for the Law to Israel, what God's son's ransom really bought, and what the New Covenant was about. When you know the answers to the questions, you can understand this chapter. All the quotes I use from the Bible are from Jay P. Green's translation as it has the Hebrew language as well as the English translation. Also, the Hebrew words are cross-referenced with *Strong's Concordance* numbers. The same with the Greek, but in this case I am reading from the American Standard Version, which I feel is better than most translations.

We start with 2 Corinthians 5:1, which says, "For we know that if the earthly house of our tabernacle be dissolved, we have a building from God, a house not made with hands, eternal, in the heavens." Where it says "earthly house of our tabernacle," the words "of our" is not in the Bible. It says "the earthly house" and the "tabernacle" are the same, and "building from God"[25] in 1 Corinthians 3:9 says "you are the building of God."[26] To better understand, read Ephesians 2:19–22: "So then, you are no longer strangers and tenants, but you are fellow citizens, of the Saints and of the Household of God, being built upon the foundation of the apostles and the prophets, Jesus Christ himself being the cornerstone; to whom all the building fitted together grows into a holy temple in the Lord; in whom you also are being built together into a dwelling place of God in the spirit."[27] This is speaking of the Body of Christ, his bride the church, or Household of God. But the Bible says that we as individuals are the house or temple of God. First Corinthians 6:19 says, "Or do you not know that body is a temple of the Holy Spirit in you."[28]

Another doctrine is the Trinity. When you read the history of the early church fathers, parts of the Trinity began to show up in the second century, and by the end of the fourth century, the Trinity had been developed into what it is today. I would encourage everyone to read the book *A History of Christianity* by Paul Johnson, as well as *When Jesus Became God* by Richard Rubenstein. The history of the Trinity does not have a good record. From ostracizing to wars, much blood has been spilled over the Trinity. While they believe the Trinity is three gods, there is one God, and all three gods are equal, all never having a beginning, all having the same power, and yet when we consider John 1:1–3, where we found that in the beginning the Word—or later Jesus—was "the" beginning of creation by the God—Revelation 3:14),[29] and the Word was God (or a god) and that the Word (or a god) was with the God in beginning,[30] and everything that exists came about through the Word (a god) and without the Word (or a god) nothing came about. So the Word (or Jesus) had a beginning, whereas "the" God whose name is Jehovah never had a beginning.[31] Psalms 90:2 and John 14:28 say, "You heard that I said to you, I am going away and I am coming again to you, if you loved me, you would rejoice that I said, I am going to the father, for my father is greater than I."[32]

There are scriptures which some who believe in the Trinity like to quote, so I will share one with you. It is Hebrews 1:8 which says, "But as to the Son, your throne, O God, is forever and ever, a scepter of righteousness is the scepter of your Kingdom." Now let us read it in the Greek language. It reads "But to the Son, O'throne of you the God is to the ages of the ages." What this is showing is "the" God is the throne that the Son sits on, or that the Son sits with his Father. What a difference, for one is deception and the other is the truth, and remember the truth will set you and me free.[33] Just another religious teaching to deceive mankind.

There are two more scriptures I would like to read to you. The first one is 1 John 4:1–3, which says, "Beloved, do not believe every spirit, but test the spirits, whether they are from God; for many false prophets have gone forth into the world, by this know the Spirit of God: every spirit which confesses that Jesus Christ has come in the flesh is from God. And every spirit which does not confess that Jesus Christ has in the flesh is not from God; and this the antichrist which you heard is coming, and now is already in the world." By the way, these who believe in the Trinity have to believe God simply materialized in flesh, which means a perfect human life was not given for the life of the world of mankind.[34]

The other scripture is 2 John 7, which says, "Because many deceivers went out into the world, those not confessing Jesus Christ to have come in the flesh." The last part from the Greek language says "those not confessing Jesus Christ coming in the flesh."[35] The word "coming" is in *Strong's Concordance* cross-reference number 2064.[36] In 1 John 4:1–3, the word "coming" is in the past tense, but the "coming" in 2 John 7 is spelled differently; the first four letters are EPXO, and every time "coming" appears in the Greek scriptures spelled in that way, it means either present tense or future tense but never past tense.[37] Jesus did not come then, so it has to be future, and Matthew 24:30 says, "And then the sign of the Son of Man will appear in the heavens, and then all tribes of the land will wail, and they will see the Son of Man coming on the clouds of heavens with power and much glory."[38] The word "coming" is spelled the same as the word "coming" in 2 John 7, and we know that refers to the future.

Anyone who does not believe that Jesus is coming in the flesh is following the Antichrist, so you can see that Satan truly has deceived the whole world. I hope this study will help all of us in following "the Christ" by eliminating the antibeliefs with the beliefs of the Christ. Jehovah "the God" will not desert us if we ask him to help us in following "Christ." Just another religious teaching to deceive mankind.

May Jehovah bless us all as we do our best to follow "the Christ."

Chapter 3

The Resurrection of Jesus to Life As?

Isaiah 9:6-7 prophesied about Jesus, saying, "For a child is born to us a son is given; and the government is on his shoulder and his name is called wonderful, Counselor, the mighty God, the everlasting father, the prince of peace. There is no end to the increase of his government and peace on the throne of David, and on his Kingdom, to order it, and to sustain it with justice and righteousness, from now and forever the zeal of Jehovah of hosts will do this."[1]

So we are talking about a kingdom, with a government and a king sitting on the throne of King David. It also speaks about the expansion of this government as it fills the earth.

Acts 2:29-32 speaks about the beginning of the fulfillment of that prophecy, saying, "Men, brothers, it is permitted to say to you with plainness as to the patriarch David, that he both died and was buried, and his tomb is among us until this day. Being a prophet, then, and knowing that God swore with an oath to him that of the fruit of his loin, as concerning flesh, to raise the Christ to set on his throne; Therefore it seems he spoke about the resurrection of the Christ, that his soul was not left in Hades, nor did his flesh see corruption. This Jesus, God raised up, as we are all witnesses."[2]

What we just read says that Jesus is mighty God, everlasting Father, and Prince of Peace, and that he will sit of David's throne, and that his flesh will never see corruption, or that the man Jesus will be the King of God's kingdom on this earth forever.

But here is a problem scripture, 1 Peter 3:18–19, which says Jesus became a spirit. It says, "Because Christ once suffered concerning sins, the just for the unjust, that he might bring us to God; indeed being put to death in the flesh, But made alive in the spirit, in which also, going in to the spirits in prison, He then proclaimed."₃ If the verse seems to say that Jesus was made spirit, then all the scriptures that we have read are confusing us. For example, Acts 2:31–32 says, "Foreseeing, he spoke about the resurrection of the Christ, that his soul was not left in Hades,(or grave) nor did his flesh see corruption. This Jesus, God raised up, of which we are all witnesses."₄ The word "soul" means breathing creature, or body. If Jesus became spirit, then his flesh or body did see corruption, meaning it went back to the ground, and Timothy 2:5 says, "For God is one, also there is one mediator of God and of men, the man Christ Jesus."₅ Thus, after the resurrection, there would be no mediator, and the man Christ Jesus no longer exists, and the Bible is just confusing us and leaving us with no sure hope.

Thank God, our father Jehovah, that's not what 1 Peter 3:18 says. Let's look at P.S. Green's translation, the Greek to English with *Strong's Concordance* references, and see what it says. "Indeed being put to death truly in flesh, But made alive the spirit; in which also the in prison spirits going he proclaimed."₆ Notice that it does not say "made alive in the spirit" but "made alive the spirit," so the spirit of Jesus was made alive. To help us understand, let's read Acts 7:59, where it says, "And they stoned Stephen, invoking and saying, Lord Jesus, receive my spirit."₇ In Luke 23:42–43, the thief on the cross next to Jesus said, "Lord remember me when you come into your Kingdom, and Jesus said to him, truly I say to you today, you will be with me in paradise."₈ And Luke 33:46 says, "And crying with a loud voice, Jesus said, Father, into your hands I commit my spirit."₉ If someone mentioned the name of a person, you see the person in the mind's eye, and you see if he or she is kind, gentle, devious, strong, weak, honest, boastful, generous, or not. That's his or her spirit, not your soul. Luke 1:46–47 says, "And Mary said, my soul magnifies the lord, and my spirit exulted in God my savior."₁₀ So you can see, the soul is you, and your spirit is what you are. So when Stephen, the thief, and Jesus asked that their spirit be received or remembered, their soul could be made alive because their spirit tells the one making alive what they are. When God made alive the spirit of Jesus, he made the soul Jesus alive, because the spirit told God what Jesus was. Next, it says in which the word "in" is in *Strong's* reference number 1722 and means "position"—"in place, time, or state." Since it's speaking of the resurrection of Jesus, the phrase is "in state,"[11] which is in *Strong's* reference number 3739, and in this case it's spelled w; I checked that spelling all through the Greek, and it's translated most of the time as "whom," and which the other times, in this case, since it is speaking of the resurrected state of Jesus, it should say whom.[12] So that scripture really is saying, "Because even Christ once suffered concerning sins, the just for the unjust, that he might bring you to God; indeed being put to death in the flesh, But made alive the spirit, in whom also, going in to the spirits in prison, he the proclaimed. But I said "resurrected state," you remember; if you make the spirit alive, the soul is made alive, meaning the man Jesus. Now 1 John 3:2 says, "Beloved, now we are children of God, and it was not yet revealed what we shall be. But we know that if he should be revealed, we shall be like him because we shall see him as he is."[13] But what did John know about what Jesus was? Now we already know that Acts 2:31 tells us that his soul was not left in Hades, nor did his flesh see corruption,[14] nor that his body became alive, and 1 Timothy 2:5 says that Jesus the man would be mediator between God and men; after the one-thousand-year reign of Christ, the resurrection of mankind will happen, and they will have the mediator Christ Jesus the man. So John knew that Jesus would be a perfect man. But when Jesus was resurrected that evening, according to John 20:19–20, "then it being evening on that day, the first of the week, and the door having been locked, where the disciples were assembled, because of the fear of the Jews, Jesus came and stood in the midst of them and said peace to you. And saying this, he showed them his hands and side, then seeing the Lord, the disciples rejoiced."[15] Did you notice that Jesus had the ability to go into the invisible and into the visible at will? Now whether a man can do this John did not know. And when anybody tells you that they know, then they are saying they know more than the apostle John. I think we can safely say that no one knows what we will be; perfect man and woman, yes, but beyond that, we don't know. We do know that mankind's future is not in heaven, but on the earth! So we will be men and women.

Why not review Jesus's resurrection as a man, a spirit, or in whatever form it might turn out to be? Isaiah 9:6–7 clearly shows that Jesus will rule on David's throne as a mighty God, Prince of Peace, and that government and kingdom will be on the earth.[16]

We found out that Jesus was resurrected a man and that his flesh will never see corruption, which means he will be a man forever, then we considered 1 Peter 3:18, where Jesus was made alive in the spirit.

After going over that scripture, we found that the spirit of Jesus was made alive, we found the spirit is what you are, and there is comfort in this knowledge because, while none of us remember the spirit of anyone who lived five thousand years ago, Jehovah the God and Father of Jesus has received the spirit of everyone who lived, so he remembers them and will resurrect them. Acts 24:15 says "a resurrection of both the just and unjust." That's why Jesus, as he was dying, asked his father Jehovah to receive his spirit.[17]

So we can say that Jesus will be a man forever, but what else is he? 1 John 3:2 says we don't know, but we do know that the man Jesus had the ability to go into the visible and the invisible at will; we don't know what you call that. At the resurrection we will know. First Corinthians 3:18–22 says, "Let no one deceive himself if anyone thinks to be wise among you in this age, Let him become foolish, that he may become wise. For the wisdom of this world is foolishness with God; for it has been written, "He takes the wise in their own craftiness." And again, "The Lord knows the reasoning of the wise, that they are worthless." So let no one glory in men; for all things are yours, whether Paul, or Opollos, or Cephas, or the world, or life, or death, or things present, or things to come. *All are yours*, and you are Christ's and Christ is God's. "That is Jehovah."[18]

So when you look at *Earth* and the *Universe*, with all of its potential, remember it's all yours! *What a future!*

Chapter 4

The Abrahamic Covenant

To the reader of this article: I hope to show how the subject "the Abrahamic Covenant," a covenant found throughout the Bible, reveals God's divine purpose to all mankind. As to the purpose God planned before the foundation of the world, read 1 Peter 1:19–20

The Abrahamic Covenant

Abraham left Ur of the Chileans as God commanded and went to Land of Canaan, and from there, the Abrahamic Covenant evolved. Please read Genesis chapters 12–22:5 to understand the sequence of events,[73] then read Genesis 22:6–18, where it says, "And Abraham took the wood of the burnt offering and laid it on his son Isaac; and he took the fire and the knife in his hand, and the two went together, and Isaac spoke to his father Abraham and said, my father, and he said, Behold me, and he said, see the fire and the wood! But where is the lamb for a burnt offering? And Abraham said, my son, God will provide himself a lamb for a burnt offering, and the two of them went together, and they came to the place which God had said to him, and Abraham built there the altar, and arranged the wood, and he bound his son Isaac and laid him on the altar, on the wood, and Abraham stretched out his hand and took the knife to slay his son, and the Angel of Jehovah called to him from the heavens and said, Abraham, and he said, behold me, and he said, Do not lay your hand on the boy, nor do anything to him, for now I know you are a God fearer, and you have not withheld your son, <u>your only one,</u> from me. And Abraham lifted up his eyes and looked, and behold! A ram behind him was entangled in a thicket by his horns, and Abraham went and took the ram and offered him a burnt offering instead of his son. And Abraham called the name of that place Jehovah will see; so that it is said until this day, in the Mount of Jehovah it will be seen. and the Angel of Jehovah called to Abraham out of the heavens a second time. and he said I have by myself, declares Jehovah, that on account of this thing you have done, and not have withheld your son, your only son, that blessing I will bless you, and multiplying I will multiply your seed like the stars of the heavens and as the sand which is on the seashore, And your seed shall possess the gate of his enemies, And in your seed shall all the nations of the Earth shall be blessed as reward in that you have obeyed my voice."[74]

Now if you have read Genesis chapters 12 through 22, you know that Abraham's faith was not a blind faith. Hebrews 11:1 states, "Now faith is the substance of things hoped for, the evidence of things not being seen."[75] The reference number for substance in *Strong's Concordance* is number 5287. It states "a setting under (support) essence – assurance."[76] You can add "substance." A setting gives support for what we hope for; you cannot see it, but we have faith that we will acquire it. For example, Babalon was destroyed, and the Israel of God was set free, and the temple was rebuilt, just as God's Word had said, and the seed of Abraham did come; his name was Jesus, and he did give his life for the world of mankind. These are all the "substance" that gives us faith that Jesus will come in kingdom power and bring peace to the earth and eternal life to the world of mankind.

If you will go back to Genesis 17 where it tells about the sign between Jehovah and Abraham over the covenant, it states in Genesis 17:10–11 that "this is the Covenant which you shall keep, between me and you, your seed after you: Every man-child among you shall be circumcised. And you shall circumcise the flesh of your foreskin, and it shall be a token of the Covenant between me and you."[77] (The word "token" also means signal, evidence, and sign.) In *Strong's Concordance*, the reference number is 226.[78]

Circumcision also became a part of the law covenant given to the Israelites 430 years later. Read Exodus 12:44, where it says, "But where there is any slave man purchased with money, you must circumcise him. Then first he may share in eating it." (He was speaking about the Passover.)[79] And Galatians 5:3 says, "And I testify again to every man being circumcised, that he is a debtor to do all the law."[80] So circumcision is a part of the Abrahamic Covenant and the Law Covenant. And when the seed arrived that ended circumcision and the Law Covenant, Galatians 3:24 says "so that the law has become a trainer of us until Christ, that we might be justified by faith."[81]

So when Jesus came, the Law Covenant ended, and circumcision under the Abrahamic Covenant ended also. You see, when Christ Jesus came, he was the seed that the Abrahamic Covenant had promised; that part of the covenant was over. Galatians 3:16 states, "But the promises were spoken to Abraham and to his seed - it does not say, and to seeds as of many: but as of one. And to your seed which is Christ".[82]

But there is a lot more for the Abrahamic Covenant to do. We will come back to this point later, but for now, let's go back to when Abraham attempted to sacrifice Isaac his son, for there is a picture of something far greater, in another article where I explained John 3:16, which states "God gave his only begotten son."[83] This is only in the translations into English that says "only begotten" is not in the Bible. The apostate church in 325 AD begins to introduce the Trinity. They said that the Father and the Son were equal, both were God, and these two gods decided that the second god, before the age of the ages, would be in regeneration to be the son of God, and yet be God; the word they used for regeneration is "begotten," in reference number 1080 in *Strong's*[84] *Concordance*, and means a man and woman having a child; it can mean rescued from death and regeneration. The Greek word used in John 3:16 is "only born" or "sole," which means God, before anything else came into existence, gave birth to the *Word* of God.

And Revelation 3:14 reads "In the beginning of creation,"[85] so you can see why the apostate church could not quote John 3:16 with its true meaning, so they inserted the word "begotten," and then in 381 AD, they added the Holy Spirit to make it the Trinity and did deceive all of Christendom. Hebrews 11:17 states, "Being tested, Abraham by faith offered up Isaac; and he receiving the promises was offering up only-begotten."[86] *Strong's* number for reference is 3439, and instead of "only begotten," it says "only born,"[87] and in Genesis 22:16 and says "only son"[88] and *Strong's* reference number here is 3173 and means "only son," the reason being Sarah only gave birth to one child, making Isaac "only born," which is a picture of God giving his *only born* son as a ransom for all mankind.[89]

Next, we need to look at what happened at Sinai, the mountain where Jehovah gave the Law Covenant to Israel, all twelve tribes of them. And it was there that Jehovah gave the promise in Exodus 19:5–6, which says, "And now if you will surely listen to my voice, and will keep my Covenant, you shall become a special treasure to me above all the nations, for all the Earth is mine. And you shall become a kingdom of priests for me, A holy nation."$_{90}$ If the Israelites had kept God's Law until Jesus came, then the church, bride of Christ, or government would have been made of fleshly Israel, the seed Christ came from was the tribe of Judah. But all twelve tribes would have made the church and/or government.

But you see, they were not faithful, and the ten tribes were rejected, and no one knows what happened to them. The tribes of Judah and Benjamin went into captivity in Babylon in 586 BC and never had a king after that and stayed in trouble until Christ came. So you can see why God continued to put up with Judah until Christ came; it was because the seed of Abraham came through Judah. Even though the tribe Judah was not loyal, the seed was produced through that lineage. But they did not get the promise that they would make up the Holy Nation, the church, or bride; only a remnant of Israel made up a part of the church, or bride, for us to understand the Abrahamic Covenant.

We need to understand the Israelites' standing with Jehovah. The ten tribes of Israel we do not even know what happened to them. Judah and Benjamin continued until AD 70, and now they are a religion and are called Jews. Now some think they have a future when Jesus returns, but let's see what Jesus said on that subject.

Matthew 23:37–39 states, "Jerusalem, Jerusalem, the one killing the prophets and stoning those who have been sent to her. How often I would have gathered your children together in the way a bird gathers her chicks from under wings! And you did not desire it. Behold, your house is left to you desolate. For I say to you, in no way shall you see me from now on until you say, Bless is he who comes in the name of the Lord."$_{91}$ This is quoting from Psalms 118:26, which states, "Blessed is he who comes in the name of Jehovah; we blessed you from the house of Jehovah." So we can see that it says "Blessed is he who comes in the name of Jehovah" and then it adds "we blessed you from the house of Jehovah,"$_{92}$ and that was when Israel was the house of Jehovah. The Jews of today do not use the name Jehovah.

And today what is a Jew? Romans 2:28–29 reads "for he is not a Jew that is one outwardly, nor is circumcision that outwardly in flesh; But he is a Jew that is one inwardly; and circumcision is of heart, in spirit, now in letter, of whom the praise is not from men, But from God."[93] So how does God view the Jews of today? The same as he does the Gentiles—he loves them all. Romans 11:30–32 says, "For as you also disobeyed God, But now have obtained mercy by the disobedience of these; so also these now have disobeyed, so that they also may obtain mercy by your mercy. For God shut up all in disobedience, that he may show mercy to all."[94]

So by the disobedience of the Jews, some of the Gentiles received mercy and became part of the church and will show mercy to the Jews, and the Gentiles you remember it says, God shut them all up in disobedience, that's Jews and Gentiles. God through Jesus and the bride or church will show mercy to them all. In Exodus 19, Jehovah told the Israelites that they would be obedient to him, that they would become a special treasure to him above all the nations and become a kingdom of priests for him—a Holy Nation![95]

Now we found out that only a remnant of Israel became a part of this Holy Nation, and the rest have come from the Gentiles. The Bible says that these are a special treasure for Jehovah. Most think that Jehovah loves this Holy Nation, bride, or church more than the rest of mankind. But notice what it says, that the Holy Nation, church, or bride or special treasure has since become a kingdom of priests for Jehovah. Now we know that Jesus is the High Priest, and now we see that the Holy Nation or church is under priests to the High Priest Jesus. Most people think that the Holy Nation, bride, or church is a very large number of people, but look at Luke 12:32, for it states, "Stop being afraid, Little flock, because your Father was pleased to give you the Kingdom."[96] So we know that the number of the church, or bride, or Holy Nation is a small number. Revelation 14:1–8 says, "And I saw, and behold, the lamb standing on Mount Zion! And with him were a hundred forty-four thousands, having the name of his father written on their foreheads. And I heard a sound out of Heaven as a sound of many waters, and as sound of great thunder, also I heard a sound of harpers harping on their harps. And they sing as a new song before the throne, and before the four living creatures and the elders. And no one was able to learn the song except the hundred forty-four thousands, those having been redeemed from the earth. These are the ones who were not defiled with women, for they are virgins, these are the ones following the lamb where ever he may go. These were redeemed from among men as first-fruit to God and to the lamb and no guile was found in their mouth, for they are without blemish before the throne of God. And I saw another angel flying in mid-heaven, having an everlasting gospel to proclaim to those dwelling on the earth, even to every nation and tribe and tongue and people, saying in a great voice, Fear God, and give glory to him, because the hour of his judgment has come; and worship him who has made the heaven, and the earth, and the sea, and the fountains of waters." "And another angel followed, saying, the great city Babylon, has fallen, has fallen; because of the wine of the anger of her fornication, she has made all nations to drink."

You remember Luke said, "Fear not little Flock, for the father has approved of giving you the kingdom." We now know the Bible says 144,000; next, they are not defiled with women, for they are virgins. This is speaking of women as religions of the world, and all have been misled, and I think most of the 144,000 were part of at least one of these religions, but these have been born from above, and 1 Corinthians 5:17 says, "So that if anyone is in Christ, that one is a new creation; the old things have passed away, behold, all things have become new!"[26] And then it says these are first fruits to God and to the lamb. That means that there are more fruits to come, most of the world of mankind! The fourteenth chapter of Revelation gives us a sense of where we are in the stream of time. Verse 7 says, "Saying in a Great voice, Fear God, and give glory to him because the hour of his judgment has come; and worship him who has made the heaven, and the earth, and the sea, and the fountains of waters." And verse 8 says, "And another angel followed saying, the great city Babylon, has fallen, has fallen because of the wine of the anger of her fornication, she has made all nations to drink."[27] The wine in this scripture pictures the false beliefs of Christendom that these religions have made mankind drink. Deuteronomy 32:32–33 says, "For their vine is of the vine of Sodom, and their grapes of the fields of Gomorrah, grapes of Gall, they have bitter clusters. Their wine is the venom of serpents, and the cruel venom of Asps."[28] So you can see Christendom's wine is poison, the Trinity, going to heaven, soul is immortal, eternal torment, and other teachings. For example, Trinity makes Jesus one of three gods. So if that were true, then the world of mankind has *not* been purchased, and there is no hope. But thanks to Jehovah, the Trinity is just an idol and never could save anyone. We now know that Jesus was truly the son of God. Not the God. You see, if Jesus had been the God, he would be immortal and could not die. So mankind has been misled.

But some are now learning the truth. That Jesus is the beginning of creation (Revelation 3:14) and did give his life for all mankind.[29] More on the times that we live in, verse 8 says that Babylon the great has fallen[30]; I don't think that Babylon has fallen yet. Communism had no use for all religion, including Christendom. Evolution makes fun of religion, including Christendom. The Moslem extremists are a threat that's growing against Christendom, which is Babylon the Great, and those and other forces will cause her to fall and be destroyed.

Since we now can see that Babylon the Great is in danger, we know that the kingdom will take control of Earth and bring peace. The seventh chapter of Revelation helps understand the number 144,000, which is the church or bride, and also government of the kingdom. Revelation 7:1–4 says, "And after these things I saw four angels standing on the four corners of the earth, holding the four winds of the earth, that wind should not blow on the earth, nor on the sea, nor on every tree, And I saw another angel coming up from the rising of the living God. And he cried with a great voice to the four angels to whom it was given to them to harm the earth and the sea, saying, do not harm the earth, nor the sea, nor the trees, until we seal the slaves of our God on their foreheads. And I heard the number of those having been sealed: one hundred forty-four thousands; having been sealed out of every tribe of the sons of Israel."[31] You remember the twelve tribes of fleshly Israel—picture the spiritual Israel, the church, or bride of Christ Jesus.

To help us understand, this small group, the church, or bride of Christ, or government, we need to understand the new covenant. The old Law Covenant for the Israelites had ten commandments and many other laws, it had animal sacrifice administered by the Levi priesthood, and it did not cancel sin but pictured the blood of Jesus which does cancel sin. Galatians 3:19 says, "Why then the law? It was added because of transgressions until the seed should come to those in whom it had been promised."[32] Hebrews 8:10–13 quotes from Jeremiah 31, and this is what it says: "Because this is the covenant which I will covenant with the house of Israel after those days, says the Lord, 'Jehovah' giving my Laws into their minds, and I will write them on their hearts, and I will be their God, and they shall no more teach each one his neighbor, and each one his brother, saying, know the Lord, because all shall know me, from the least of them to their great ones, For I will be merciful to their unrighteousness and I will not at all remember their sins and their lawless deeds. In the saying, 'new,' he has made the first old, and the thing having been old and growing aged is near disappearing."[33]

This new covenant embraces spiritual Israel. Spiritual Israel, the church, or bride of Christ plays a vital part in God's purpose for all mankind that make up the little flock. Luke 12:32 says "Stop being afraid Little Flock, because your father was pleased to give you the kingdom"$_{34}$ or church, or bride of Christ, which is 144,000 in number. How does one become a part of this little flock? No one makes that choice but the Father.

John 6:44 says, "No one is able to come to me unless the father who sent me <u>draws</u> him and I will raise him up into the last day."$_{35}$ At that time, the Father (Jehovah) adopts that person. Romans 8:15–16 says, "For you did not receive a spirit of slavery again to fear, but you received a spirit of adoption by which we cry, Abba! Father! The spirit himself witnesses with our spirit that we are children of God."$_{36}$ And since we have been turned over to Jesus, we want to be baptized into Christ Jesus.

In Romans 6:3–11, we read "or are you ignorant that all we were baptized into Christ Jesus were baptized into his death? Therefore, we were buried with him through baptism into death that as Christ was raised up from the dead by the glory of the Father, so also we should walk into newness of life. For if we have been joined together in the likeness of his death, so also shall we be in the resurrection; know this, that our old man was crucified with him, that the body of sin might be annulled, so that we no longer serve sin. For the one that died has been justified from sin. But if we died with Christ, we believe that also we shall Live with him, knowing that Christ being raised from the dead dies no more; death no longer Lords it over him, for in that he died. He died to sin once for all; But in that Lives, he Lives to God, so also you count yourself to be truly dead to sin, but alive to God, in Christ Jesus our Lord."$_{37}$ And then we are born again or better born from above. John 3:3 says, "Jesus answered, truly, truly, I say to you, if one does not receive birth out of water and spirit, he is not able to enter into the Kingdom of God."$_{38}$ Water is the Word of God; Spirit is the Holy Spirit.

Then he says in verses 6–7 "that receiving birth from the flesh is flesh; and that receiving birth from the spirit is spirit, Do not wonder because I told you, you must receive birth from above."$_{39}$ To help us better understand being born from spirit, let's read Romans 8:8–11, where it says, "And those being in the flesh are not able to please God. But you are not in flesh, but in spirit, since the spirit of God dwells in you, But if any one has not the Spirit of Christ, this one is not his. But if Christ is in you, the body indeed is dead because of sin, But the spirit is life because of righteousness. But if the spirit of the one having raised Jesus from the dead dwells in you, the one having raised the

Christ from the dead will also make your mortal bodies Live through the in dwelling of his spirit in you."$_{40}$ So if we are in spirit, we are in Christ, or in tune with Christ with our mind, and our body still is sinful in nature, But then the Bible says when Christ comes, he will make alive our mortal body! So when Jesus comes in kingdom power, all the bride of Christ, or church, according to 1 Corinthians 15:51–53, will all put on immortality, meaning the Abrahamic Covenant has produced the seed "Jesus,"$_{41}$ who in turn gave his life for the world of mankind, and the Father has adopted with the blood of Jesus the Little Flock, bride of Christ, or church, so when Jesus comes and the bride of Christ is given immortality, then Jehovah and his son Jesus will set their sights on the world of mankind!

The early part of the world of mankind is the great crowd mentioned in Revelation 7:9–17. The first part of Revelation chapter 7 deals with the angels holding the four winds of destruction, being held back until the 144,000 have been sealed; that's when Jesus returns to the earth with kingdom power and to all the good people living on the earth at that time. Revelation 7:9–17 says, "After these things I saw, and look! A great crowd, which no man was able to number, out of all the nations, and tribes and peoples and tongues, standing before the throne and before the lamb, dressed in white robes; and there were palm branches in their hands, And keep on crying with a loud voice, saying: 'Salvation we owe to our God to is seated on the throne, and to the lamb.' And all the angels were standing around the throne and the elders and the four Living creatures, and they fell upon their faces before the throne, and worshipped God, saying; Amen! The blessing and the glory and the honor and the power and the strength be to our God forever and ever, Amen! And in response one of the elders said to me: 'these who are dressed in the white robes, who are they and where did they come from?' So right away I said to him: 'My Lord, you are the one that knows.' And he said to me: 'these are the ones that come out of the great tribulation, and they have washed their robes and made them white in the blood of the lamb. That is why they are before the throne of God; and they are rendering him sacred service day and night in his temple; and the one seated on the throne will spread his tent over them. They will hunger no more nor thirst anymore, neither will the sun beat down upon them nor any scorching heat, because the lamb who is in the midst of the throne, will Sheppard them, and will guide them to fountains of waters of life, and God will wipe out every fear from their eyes.'"$_{42}$

I think we can agree that the great crowd shows up when Jesus comes in kingdom power. And many think they are in heaven, because it says they are before the throne and in his temple, but if we read carefully, we find the great crowd are not *saved* people, at that time they are accepting the blood of Jesus by washing their robes white in the blood of Jesus and they are being lead to fountains of waters of life. Isaiah 6:1 says, "Heaven is my throne and the Earth is my foot stool."[43] So that puts them before the throne, and I have shown in my earlier writing that the church, or bride, make up the Body of Christ and that is the temple of God, at that time the bride will be complete and working with their husband Jesus in behalf of the great crowd here on Earth! This is during the one-thousand-year rule of Christ and the church, or bride. At the end of the one-thousand-year rule, the old heavens and earth are no more. Then Jehovah and his son Jesus will be ready for the resurrection of the world of mankind. So during the one-thousand-year rule, the earth will be turned into a paradise, and you remember Jesus promised the thief on the stake next to him that he would be with him (Christ) in paradise. So we can see that the great crowd is the early part of the world of mankind! Everything that Jehovah and Jesus have done so far is getting ready for the resurrection of the world of mankind with Jehovah and Jesus in kingdom power, which I think is very close. Now I can't say when that will be, but Bible prophecy tells us that it is close. One example is Matthew 24:21–22, which says, "For there will be great affliction, 'tribulation' such as has not happened from the beginning of the world until now. And except those days had been shortened, not any flesh would be saved- But on account of the elect, those days will be shortened."[44] I think the tribulation started in 325 AD when the church became apostate and began fighting against the seed, or the true Christians.

Revelation 17:6 says, "And I saw the woman being drunk from the blood of the Saints, and from the Blood of the witnesses of Jesus."[45] Other prophecies indicate that the terrorist that we see coming are coming against all Christendom and, I think, also the Jewish state. With the nuclear weapons they will soon have, I think you can see that if this tribulation is not cut short, no flesh would be saved. We need to talk about the woman used to picture the Abrahamic Covenant. The first one is found in Genesis 3:15, which says, "And I will put enemy between you and the woman, and between your seed and her seed- He will bruise you in the head and you will bruise him in the heel."[46] What that is saying is that the woman will cause a bruising of Satan and his seed in the head, and his seed will only be able to bruise the woman's seed on the heel.

The next woman is described in the twelfth chapter of Revelation. This event happens at Pentecost.[47] You can read about Pentecost in the twenty-third chapter of Leviticus; after the seventh Sabbath, you count fifty days from Passover to Pentecost where they offer to Jehovah a great offering. On this day, Jesus was to baptize them with the Holy Spirit.[48] Read Acts 1:4–5. This means gifts of prophecy, tongues, and some could even resurrect people back to life.[49] Now most people think this is when they—the church, or bride of Christ—were born again, but that's not true; the day Jesus was resurrected, that evening he had already appeared before Jehovah with his sacrifice and was now meeting with the church, or bride. You remember that morning Jesus did not allow Mary to touch him; Jesus said that he had not ascended to his father, but that evening, he invited his disciples to touch him. Then, John 20:21–23 states, "Jesus said to them again, Peace to you, As the father has sent me, I also send you, and saying this, He breathed on them, and said to them, receive the holy spirit of whomever you forgive the sins, they are forgiven to them, or whomever you may retain, they are retained."[50] So you see they could act as priests after they were born from above. Concerning the gifts they got at Pentecost, the only way those gifts of the Holy Spirit could be passed on was through the laying on the hand of an apostle, which meant that the gifts of the Holy Spirit came to an end. Read it in Acts 19:6 so you can see that Pentecost was the birth of the church, or bride of Christ.[51] And you will now see how the woman in the twelfth chapter of Revelation played her part. Revelation 12:1–2 says, "And a great sign was seen in heaven, a woman having been clothed with the sun, and the moon was underneath her feet; And on her head a crown of twelve stars; and having a babe in womb, she cries, being in labor, and having been distressed to bear."[52] As you can see, all creation, "except for Satan and his demons," are in tune with the woman.

Next, we see the great red dragon having seven heads and ten horns, and on his heads were seven (crowns). And his tail drew the third part of the stars of the heaven, and he throws them to the earth. Next, it shows the dragon standing before the woman to devour her child. Then it says she bore a son, a male, who is going to shepherd all the nations with an iron staff, and her child was caught away to God and to his throne, and the woman fled into the wilderness, where she has a place, it having been prepared from God, that there they might nourish her for 1,260 days.

Next, it shows war in heaven, with Michael and his angels waging war against the dragon. And the dragon and his angels make war. But Satan did have the strength to stay in heaven, so he and his angels were cast out to the earth. Then it says, "Now has come the salvation and power and the kingdom of our God, and the authority of his Christ. Because the accuser of our brothers is thrown down, the one accusing them before our God day and night, and they overcame him because of the blood of the lamb, and because of the word of their testimony, and they did not love their soul even until death." You noticed the serpent casting a third of the demons to the earth; I think that was done when Jesus, the seed, came to the earth, and the demons were plentiful at that time, and they had a job to do. But after Satan and his demons were cast out into the earth, the heavens were rid of them. After the dragon saw he was cast out of heaven, he pursued the woman who bore the male, and two wings of a great eagle were given to the woman to fly away into the wilderness, where she is fed there a time and times and half a time, away from the serpent's face, then the serpent threw water out of his mouth, that the woman might be carried off by the river, but the earth opened its mouth and swallowed the river. You see when the woman bore a son, a male, which is the church, or bride, from the hands of Jesus came salvation and power and the kingdom of our God and the authority of his Christ.

So the woman's job was finished after the 1,260 years; then the woman will give birth to the salvation of the great crowd, which is the early part of the world of mankind which has always been the apple of God's eye. Since the woman's job is finished, she is no longer prominent and soon fades away, so Satan's words of hate the earth swallows up. But that means that the kingdom of God came at Pentecost. Yes, Colossians 1:12–13 says, "Giving thanks to the Father, who has made us fit for a share of the inheritance of the Saints in Light, who delivered us out of the power of darkness, and translated us into the kingdom of the son of his love."$_{53}$ So since Pentecost, the birth of the church, or bride of Christ, they were transformed into the kingdom of the son of his love. In the very near future, that kingdom will take in the whole earth. And it will rule for a thousand years, and after that the resurrection of the whole world of mankind will take place, and then Jehovah will bless all nations of the earth through the seed of Abraham! And this concludes the Abrahamic Covenant. Just as the old Law Covenant accomplished its purpose and came to an end, so will the Abrahamic Covenant come to its end, but before we end this article, we have another view of the woman, and it's found in Galatians 4:22–26, which says, "Abraham had two sons, one out of the slave-woman, and one out of the free woman, But indeed, he of the slave-woman has been born according to flesh; and he of the free-woman through the promise; which things are being allegorized; for these are two covenants, one indeed, from Mount Sinai bringing forth to slavery-which is Hagar, for Hagar is Mount Sinai in Arabia, and corresponds to the present Jerusalem, and she is in slavery with her children. But the Jerusalem from above is free, who is the mother of us all!"[54] Jerusalem was the capital city, and the Abrahamic Covenant is the control part of Jehovah's divine purpose. And that woman is the mother of us all.

The Jerusalem above is also called Heavenly Jerusalem, as described in Hebrews 12:22 where it says, "But you are drawn near to Mount Zion, even the City of the living God, to a Heavenly Jerusalem, and to myriads of angels."[55] Jehovah's organization or government—that is the mother of us all.

Chapter 5

Who Is the God? Who Is the Great Idol?

Revelation 12:9 says Satan has "misled the habitable world." How many people think they have been misled? Not many, and yet the Bible says the whole world has been misled; thus, a reasonable person would have to say that Satan has done a good job.[1]

The pharisees of Jesus's day is a good example. John 8:38–44 says, "I speak what I have seen with my father, and you therefore do what you have seen with your father. They answered and said to him, Abraham is our father. Jesus said to them, if you were children of Abraham, you would do the works of Abraham, but now you seek to kill me, a man that has spoken the truth to you, which I heard alongside God. Abraham did not do this. You do the works of your father. They said to him, we were not born of fornication; we have one father, God, then Jesus said to them, if God were your Father, you would love me, for I went forth and have come from God, for I have not come from myself, but that one sent me. Why do you not understand my speech? It is because you are not able to hear my word. You are of the Devil as father, and the lusts of your father you desire to do. That one was a murderer from the beginning, and he has not stood in the truth because there is no truth in him, when he speaks a lie, he speaks from his own because he is a liar, and the father of it."[2]

These people hated God's son so much that they put him to death and allowed Satan to become their God! The hatred they had for God's son made it easy for Satan to deceive them.

A large number or most of mankind is not guilty of this kind of hatred, and I feel these are people who are aware of the aging process and that it leads to death; that's why they belong to all the religions that make up Christendom. They know something about Jesus Christ, and they know they cannot save themselves, so they do the best they can. They don't really know what will happen after death and who Jesus really is. I have written an article about who the Christ is, so please get it and read it. And most do not know who the Father is; that is what this article is about.

Many people think that God is really three gods and yet one God. No one can explain it. I want to introduce the God. Mark 12:29–30 says, "And Jesus answered him. The first of all the commandments is; Hear, Israel. The Lord our God is one Lord and you shall love the Lord, your God with all your heart, and with all your soul, and with all your strength, this the first commandment."[3]

One means one, not three in one; you can use the word "one" as one "another" meaning a group of people get along with one another, but in all cases it means one. *Strong's Concordance* number is 1520. Look it up.[4]

To help us to further understand who God is, let us look at the word "the." In John 1:1, we read "In the beginning was the Word, and the Word with God, and the Word was God."[5] Now that sure looks like God and the Word are the same or one. Right? But that's a translation of the Bible. Now let us look at the Greek-to-English to see what it says. It starts with "in the beginning," and the Greek just says "In beginning," not "in the beginning." The beginning is at Revelation 3:14: "these things says the Amen, the faithful and the true witness. The beginning of the creation of God."[6] That is before the universe was created that God gave birth to his only born Word, who is spirit, not a he or she, but it, and *Strong's Concordance* reference number 848 can mean he, she, or it inasmuch as the word was "spirit," not a she or he, not male or female. So the Word is "it."[7]

Now let us read John 1:14: "And the Word became flesh and tabernacles among us and we beheld the glory of him, Glory as of an only born from the father, full of grace and truth."[8] When the Word became flesh, a male (*Strong's* reference number 848) now becomes a "him"; when he became flesh, he became Jesus, the only born son of God.

Now note John 1:1–3 as it states more correctly in English: "In a beginning was the Word, and the Word was with the God, and a God was the Word. It was in a beginning with the God. All things came into being through it, and without it not even one thing came into being that has come into being." Now verses 4 and 5 move forward in time to when the Word became flesh and tabernacles among us, or mankind. So it becomes a "him," and it says, "In him was life, and the life was the light of man, and the light shines in the darkness, and the darkness did not overtake them."[9] The "them," as in *Strong's* reference number 848, is speaking of mankind that believed in Jesus, and so they are the light! Now we have found out that Jesus is "a God," and according to John, in the eighth chapter, Satan is "a God," and there are many more.[10]

In 1 Corinthians 8:5–6, we find a very important truth: "For even if some are called Gods either in heaven or on the earth, even as there are many Gods, and many Lords, but to us is one God, the Father, of whom are all things, and we for him, and one Lord Jesus Christ, through whom are all things, and we by him."[11] It means that through Jesus we have approach to the God, and all the things are from the God.

Another truth about the God is in Psalms 90:2: "Before the mountains were born, or ever you had formed the Earth and the world; even from everlasting to everlasting you are God."[12] And we know according to John 3:16 that the God sent his only born son into the world that everyone believing into him should not perish but have eternal life.[13] "Only begotten" is not in the Bible. It is "only born" and means "only born" or "sole," which means that God gave birth to only one, whom we know as Jesus, who had a beginning. The father or "the God" had no beginning.

Here is another truth about the God. First Kings 8:27 says, "But will God in truth dwell on the earth? Behold, the heavens and the heavens of the heavens cannot contain you. How much less this house which I have built!"[14] What he is saying is that God is bigger than the universe, and anywhere you go, God is there.

Another truth about God is his greatness. Isaiah 46:9–10 says, "Remember former things from forever, for I am God, and no one else is God, even none like me. Declaring the end from the beginning."[15] An example is found in 1 Peter 1:19–20: "But with precious blood of Christ, as an unblemished and unspotted lamb, indeed having been foreknown before the foundation of the world, but revealed in the last times because of you."[16] What this is saying is that God and the Word knew that the first Adam would lose sonship in sin and that the Word would become flesh (John 1:14) and be known as Jesus the Christ, the second Adam, the son of God. God loved us (Adam's children) before we came into being and, through Jesus (known then as the Word), made salvation a gift to us![17]

Now it is time for Matthew 28:19–20. It reads "And coming up Jesus talked with them saying, 'All authority in Heaven and earth was given to me. Therefore go disciple all nations, baptizing them into the name of the Father, and of the son and of the Holy Spirit.'"[18] People are to be baptized in the name of all three, but we find that only the Father and the Son have a name, so it is not a matter of pronouncing the name of each one; the Holy Spirit has no name. And we find Jesus had all authority given to him from the Father, so we can see they are not equal gods! But name means authority; character is in *Strong's* reference number 3686, or we could say the state of each one. Name of the Father the source of all energy, authority, and love; name of the Son—everything is through him; that's why Jesus said all authority was given to him, and he is the image of the Father—and name of Holy Spirit, the power of God, which can do anything God wants.[19] An example is with Samson in Judges 15:14, which says, "And he came to Lehi, and the Philistines shouted to meet him. And the Spirit of Jehovah came upon him, and the thick cords, which were on his arms were as flax, which they burn with fire. And his bonds melted from his hands."[20] So the Spirit does whatever the Father's will is, and Jesus the son of God can use God's spirit also. So when one is baptized, they know what part these names play in their salvation!

There is more to know about the Father and Son. Start with the Father who is the source of all energy. Isaiah 40:26 uses in various translations: dynamic energy, great in strength, vital in power, great in power. I think I can agree that God is the source of all energy.[21] He also is the source of love; 1 John 4:16 says, "God is Love." God never had a beginning; Psalms 90:2 says, "Everlasting to Everlasting." God is immortal;[22] 1 Timothy 6:16 says "the only one having immortality."[23] He could not have died to ransom mankind![24] And the God has a name; Psalms 83:18 says, "And let them know-your name is Jehovah-that you alone are the most high over All the Earth."[25] Add Deuteronomy 6:4, which says, "Hear, O Israel, Jehovah our God is one Jehovah, and you shall Love Jehovah your God with all your heart, and with all your soul, and with all your might."[26] Jesus quotes this scripture in Mark 12:29–30. So we know that God is not three but one God.[27]

Many people know the name but not the meaning of his name. Exodus 6:3 says, "And I appeared to Abraham, to Isaac, and to Jacob as God Almighty, and by my name Jehovah I never made myself known to them." Now let us read Genesis 17:1, where it states, "And when Abraham was ninety-nine years old, Jehovah appeared to Abraham and said to him, I am the Almighty God! Walk before me and be perfect."[28] Abraham knew that it was Jehovah speaking to him. He thought of him as Almighty God, which is not the meaning of his name. Exodus 3:13–15 says, "And Moses said to God, Behold, I shall come to the sons of Israel and say to them, the God of your Fathers has sent me to you; And they will say to me, what is his name? What shall I say to them? And God said to Moses, I am that I am, and he said, you shall say this to the sons of Israel, Jehovah the God of your Fathers, the God of Abraham, the God of Isaac, and the God of Jacob, has sent me to you. This is my name forever, and this is my title from generation to generation."[29]

But I'm saying this is not the meaning of God's name. *Strong's* reference number for that word is number 1961 and says "to exist, be or become, come to pass, or be" (come, accomplished).[30] Let's look at some scriptures where *Strong's* number 1961 is used; Exodus 4:9 tells us that the water taken from the Nile would become blood, so the water became blood. You remember Lot's wife? In Genesis 19:26, if she looked back, she would become a pillar of salt. She became a pillar of salt.[31] So I think you can see the Bible is saying I will become what I will become, and that is the real meaning of the name Jehovah! So what has God become? You remember we found out that before the foundation of the world, God and his son knew that Adam would be disobedient and lose life for all mankind, and John 3:16 says, "God loved the world so much that he gave his only born son, that everyone believing in him might not perish but have everlasting life."[32] What this is saying is that Jehovah loved all of us before we came into existence. He loved us and made salvation available to all of us through his son. So he has become a God of love and a God of salvation. But instead of knowing this about the great God Jehovah, Christendom has been teaching a Trinity.

Now here is a truth or a fact. The Trinity is a great idol that the apostate church introduced to the world in 325 AD and 381 AD. They said that Jesus and God were equal and the same, then in 381 AD, they added the Holy Spirit; thus, it became a Trinity. Most all of us believed they were quoting John 3:16. We were deceived. Because we now know that it does not say "only begotten" but says "only born"; we now know that before time started, God "Jehovah" gave birth to the "Word of God," and later, when Mary gave the Word a body of flesh, he became Jesus, the son of God, and "a God" was the Word. So we now know that "the Word" who later became Jesus had a beginning and cannot be "the

God." He is the "son of God," and "the God" never had a beginning, and his name is Jehovah. That is why most of the world of mankind who believe in and worship the Trinity are deceived.

Now all of us should and can worship Jehovah through Jesus. In our prayers, we need to decide if Jehovah is a friend, enemy, or our Father. If we decide on "our Father," then Jesus tells how those prayers should begin in Matthew 6:9, stating, "Our Father who is in heaven, hallowed be your name." We want to see that name "Jehovah" hallowed by all mankind, but we address him as "Father" because we are sons and daughters of God![33] This idol, the Trinity, will soon be forgotten, and we are free in Jesus Christ and through him to worship Jehovah. You remember at 1 Corinthians 3 we are told "that all things are ours," meaning the earth and the universe; they are all ours to take care of, and Jehovah and the Word, now known as Jesus, had this future for us when the universe had its beginning. Good people of the earth—this is your future!

Chapter 6

The Resurrection

It is my hope to show what the Resurrection is, what the Rapture is, and whether they are true.

I hope to show that there are two resurrections and why. Explaining how the Bible addresses these two important issues.

The Resurrection, in *Strong's Concordance* reference number 386, means "to Resurrect, raise up, rise, stand up." There are other *Strong's* numbers, such as 450 and 1453, which mean about the same, and then there is 1080 which has several meanings, such as when a woman begets a child and when she gives birth, she has begotten a child. It can also mean "to regenerate, to recover."[1] So you have Acts 13:33 where it says "that this God has fulfilled to us, their children. Raising up Jesus,[2] as also it has been written in the second Psalms: "you are my son, today I have begotten you."[3] He also raised him from the dead, not anymore about to return to corruption. Then there is number 2227, which means "to make alive, to revitalize, or to bring to life." "Resurrection" means "bring to life." However, a lot of people think that after death, the soul lives on in heaven. *Strong's* reference number 5315 (for soul) means "a breathing creature."[4] Read Genesis 1:20–21, and you will find that fish and land animals are souls.[5] Ezekiel 18:4 says the soul that sins will die.[6]

We know everyone living on Earth is guilty of sin, and by observation, we see that all of us are dying; that's why belief in the Resurrection is so important. If there were no Resurrection, there is no hope for us. Ecclesiastes 9:4–5 says, "For a living dog is better than a dead lion, for the living know that they shall die, but the dead do not know anything, nor do they have any more reward, for their memory is forgotten."[7] But thanks to our Great God whose name is Jehovah and to his only born son Christ Jesus, they do remember all of us as expressed in John 3:16: "For God so loved the world that he gave his only born son that everyone believing unto him should not perish, but have everlasting life."[8]

So there is a great future for the world of mankind. I will discuss more about this later.

Let us turn our attention to the Rapture. The book that I'm using to explain for those who believe in the Rapture is *A Quick Look at the Rapture and the Second Coming* by Tim Lahaye. Page 19 has a picture of the end of time, showing the raptured saints going to heaven, then it shows a seven-year tribulation, and then the second advent of Christ.

What that means is Jesus comes two times. Page 18 says, "We need to keep in mind that the Rapture is a signless event. There are no signs mentioned in the Bible that will indicate the Rapture is near because it is eminent, and it could happen at any moment. The Rapture cannot be related to any signs at all, thus the signs that reveal we are nearing the last days must have to do with the tribulation, a time in which God will work through Israel, and not the Church." None of this is true, as you will see.[9]

Let us now look at the Tribulation, as found in Matthew 24:15–22. It says, "Therefore, when you see the abomination of desolation which was spoken of by Daniel the prophet, standing in the Holy place, he who reads, let the reader use discernment, then let those in Judia flee to the mountains, the one on the house top, let him not come down to take anything out of the house, and the one in the fields, let him not turn back to get his garments. But woe to those that are with child and to those suckling in these days. Pray that your flight will not be in winter, nor on the Sabbath, for there will be great afflictions such as has not happened from the beginning of the world until now, no, nor ever will be. Except those days had been shortened, not any flesh would be saved, but on account of the elect those days will be shortened."[10] Some think that Luke 21:20–24 says about the same thing, but read it. It starts with Jerusalem being encircled by armies, then recognize that destruction has come near. Then it says flee to the mountains; Jerusalem will be trodden down by the nations until the times of the nations are fulfilled. Even now parts of Jerusalem are still being trodden down. For example, there is a mosque standing where Jehovah's temple used to be. So you see Luke 21 is speaking about Jerusalem, the city that has and will be trodden down until Jesus[11] comes.

Matthew 24 speaks about the church or bride of Christ. Luke chapter 21 and 70 AD are about the city itself being trodden down. Matthew 24 is about the church or bride of Christ, both pointing to the return of Jesus. Let's refer back to Matthew 24, for it mentions the abomination of desolation spoken by Daniel the prophet. I think I know where Daniel spoke about it. It's in Daniel 11:29–32: "at the appointed time he will return and come against the South, but it will not be as the former or as the latter, for ships of Kittim will come against him and he shall be grieved, and turn back, and be furious against the holy covenant, and he shall act, and return, and will heed those forsaking the holy covenants' and forces will stand from him and they will profane the sanctuary and the fortress, and they shall remove the regular sacrifice and they will place the desolating abomination."[12] The sanctuary is the house of God; it is also called the temple of God. First Peter 2:4–5 says, "Having drawn near to him, a living stone, indeed having been rejected by men, but elect precious with God, you also as living stones are being built a spiritual house, a holy priesthood to offer spiritual sacrifice acceptable to God by Jesus Christ."[13]

The king of the north is Constantine the Great, the Emperor of Rome over the west, and the emperor of the east was Licinius. In the Bible, Constantine is the king of the north, and Licinius is king of the south. There are two books that I have used among others to understand what happened during that time period; one is *When Jesus Became God* by Richard E. Rubenstein,[14] and the other is *The Age of Constantine the Great* by Jacob Burckhardt.[15] The Bible and the book about Constantine the Great describes the battle this way: "Constantine acquired, after 314 AD, significant additions to his sea power and assembled two hundred warships, Licinius, who controlled the shores of the east, had 350, the same scale obtained in other arms of service, so that Constantine had 130,000 men altogether, and Licinius 165,000." The battle happened; Constantine won with total loss of thirty-four thousand men and won the sea battle also, and Licinius lost his ships in a storm, and since this was really a civil war, you can see why, "according to the Bible: Constantine was grieved over this loss of ships." But then later, according to the book *Constantine the Great*, another land battle took place. Constantine won, and Licinius and his wife, who was Constantine's sister, asked for safety, and Constantine gave them assurance, but then a year later, he had them put to death.[16]

After the battle, the Bible says, "Constantine is furious against the holy Covenant, and he shall act, and will return, and will help those forsaking the holy Covenant. He takes side with apostates, and will profane the sanctuary, the fortress," meaning he will corrupt the sanctuary,[17] "which is the church or bride of Christ." He does this by taking sides with apostates, and they become the predominant force and "remove the regular sacrifice," which is rendering praise of Jehovah by teaching people the truth about Christ, and the kingdom of God, and the blessings to come, and so they, the apostates, with the backing of Constantine, desolate the church, or bride of Christ, by placing this abomination right in the middle of the church with the Council of Nicaea.

Let's turn our attention to the Council of Nicaea. We see in the book that when Jesus became God, Nicaea was a big lake, and Constantine owned land there and built a palace next to the lake. Constantine invited over 250 bishops and paid travel expenses and furnished rooms at the palace. Constantine used the auditorium, which was called "Judgment Hall" for the council, which started early June, 325 AD. Page 76, speaking of bishops, says "they sat on benches arranged in rows running the length of the hall, with the most distinguished churchmen occupying front row seats when all were seated. Several of the emperor's closest friends entered the room, and everyone rose, Constantine himself then appeared dressed in purple wearing the imperial diadem: a gold circlet flashing diamonds. Recognizing that he was formally a guest at the meeting, he asked the bishops permission to be seated and received a murmured assent. A small elaborately worked stool was produced, Constantine seated himself at a slight distance from the Bishops, but close enough to participate in their discussions. The bishops sat as well, and Eusebius of Caeseria arose to deliver the official welcome to the Emperor, then the Emperor gave a welcome speech. In this speech, he compared the struggle of civil war, and they should not let the evil win the war; in other words, their enemy was the true bride of Christ."[18]

First on the agenda is the Arian controversy. The Arian group did not believe in the Trinity. After about two weeks, the Arians were barred from the council. In this council, the apostates found out that they could use the Roman government's force. That's why Matthew 24:15–16 says, "Therefore when you see the abomination of desolation which was spoken of by Daniel the prophet stand in the Holy place, he who reads, let him understand, then let those in Judia flee to the mountains."[19] Notice that it let those in Judia flee. Read Romans 2:28–29, and it will tell you what a Jew is, and these were the ones who saw the abomination and fled.[20]

This is the start of the Great Tribulation. The word "tribulation" or "affliction" is in *Strong's Concordance* reference number 2347, which says "pressure afflicted, anguish, burdened, persecution, tribulation, trouble."[21] When the sons of God or the bride of Christ saw the abomination standing in the Holy Place, they fled, because they knew persecution was coming. The history of the apostate church is filled with horrible treatment of the sons of God, also fighting for the Trinity, immortal soul, going to heaven, and eternal torment. You see Satan used the apostate church in his fight against God, and since Christians say they are Christian, Satan also is using terrorism to destroy Christianity. That's why it is called the Great Tribulation. Let's now turn to Matthew 24:11–16: "and many false prophets will arise, and will mislead many. And because lawlessness shall have been multiplied, the love of many will grow cold. But the one who endures to the end, that one will be saved. And this gospel of the kingdom shall be preached in all the earth, for a testimony to all the nations, and then comes the end. Therefore, when you see the abomination of desolation which was spoken of by Daniel the prophet, standing in the Holy place, he who reads, "let him understand and then let those in Judia flee to the mountains."[22] Matthew 24:21–22 says, "For there will be great affliction, such as has not happened from the beginning of the world until now, nor ever will be and except those day had been shortened, not any flesh would be saved, but on account of the elect, those days will be shortened."[23] Today we see the terrorist groups trying to get nuclear weapons, and when they get them, they will use them, which would leave no flesh on the earth. We have discussed what leads to the Tribulation.

But then Matthew 24:23–28 covers what happens during the Tribulation and what leads to the return of Jesus and the end of the Tribulation. It says, "Then if anyone says to you, behold, here is the Christ, do not believe, for false Christ's will rise up, and false Prophets, they will give great signs and wonders, so as to lead astray, if possible, even the elect. Behold, I tell you beforehand. Then if they say to you, behold he is in the wilderness, do not go out. Behold, he is in the inner-rooms, do not believe."[24] In other words, Satan will lead with false prophets; that's why we have in Christendom so many denominations of religions. But Jesus said do not believe or go out to them. But then he said "when you see lightning flash in the east to the west," so the coming, or better, the presence of the son of men, will be in *Strong's* reference number 3952, which says "a being near, event (after return; spec, of Christ to punish Jerusalem, or finally the wicked) coming, presence."[25] It's called parousia. The people of that time were used to the political ruler visiting and area for a week or month; he lays out plans for the future and deals with local problems. That would be a parousia.

Paul used to visit congregations, and these visits were called a presence, or parousia. Read Philippians 1:26 and 2:12.[26] *Strong's* also said, "to punish Jerusalem." Jesus did speak out against the religious leaders of that time, and he will treat today's religious leaders the same. But the main purpose is to raise the dead in Christ and to gather those who are alive in Christ; that's why it then says at Matthew 24:28, "where the dead body may be, the eagles will be gathered."[27] The word "dead" is not in the Bible, just in the translation; the body of Christ and eagles, meaning members of the bride of Christ, will gather, and Christ will present them to the world. Read Matthew 24:29–31; it says, "And immediately after the affliction of those days, the sun will be darkened, and the moon will not give her light, and the stars will fall from the heavens, and the powers of the heavens will be shaken, and then the sign of the son of man will appear in the heavens, and then all the tribes of the land wail, and they will see the son of man coming in the clouds of heaven with power and much glory. He will send his angels with a great sound of a trumpet, and they will gather his elect from the four winds, from the ends of the heavens to their ends, the sun being darkened and moon not giving light, and stars falling from heaven."[28]

This pictures the governments, the politicians, and those that the people view as "stars" failing. They have no light for the future of mankind. Then we will see the sign of the son of man coming, and all tribes will wail. Why? Because the religious leaders did not prepare them for this grand event. Jesus comes to the earth for his parousia; the trumpet sound will gather the dead in Christ and those who are alive from the ends of the heavens to their ends. If you remember in Ephesians, second chapter, the elect, bride of Christ, body of Christ, are elevated to heavenly places.[29] In that time, the king Jesus with his bride the 144,000, making a righteous government, will begin the one-thousand-year rule on the earth. Now let's turn our attention to 1 Thessalonians 4:14–18: "For if we believe that Jesus died and rose again, even so God will also bring with him all those who have fallen asleep through Jesus. For we say this to you in the word of the Lord that we the living who remain to the coming of the Lord not at all will go before those who have fallen asleep, because the Lord himself shall come down from heaven with a commanding shout by an archangels voice, and with God's trumpet and the dead in Christ will rise again first, then we who remain alive will be caught up together with them in the clouds to a meeting with the Lord in the air. And so we will always be with the Lord, so then, comfort each other with these words."[30] Now I would like to read to your part of verse 15, which says "that we the living who remain to the coming of the Lord." That word, "coming," is in reference number 3952 in *Strong's Concordance* and should be translated as "presence," meaning "to come alongside," and if you remember, we found out when Paul visited the Thessalonian Church that he referred to that visit as his "presence" with them.[31]

I want to explain what I have learned about the Rapture. The ones being "caught up" are men and women, not spirits. The Rapture is an event that will take place sometime in the near future. Jesus will come in the air, to catch up the "church" from the earth, then return to heaven. This all takes place in an instant.[32] First Thessalonians 4:15 speaks about the living at the coming of the Lord. The word "coming" is referenced by number 3952 in *Strong's Concordance* and means[33] "presence" or "visit."[34] We just read about Paul visiting congregations to build them up, to instruct them in righteousness. He could be there for a week or a month. That is what Jesus will do at his presence or visit, only he will be resurrecting the dead, gather the living together in "clouds" or in groups, and introduce them to the world of mankind. If this all happened in an instant, then the Bible is wrong by saying that Jesus had a presence or visit. The Bible is not wrong, and that is why I say it is impossible that a rapture will take place.

So we can see that it's *impossible* for that event to be a *rapture*. First Corinthians 15:51–52 does speak of a change in the twinkling of the eye. Let's read what it says: "Behold I speak a mystery to you, we shall not all fall asleep, but we shall all be changed, in a moment, in a glance of an eye, at the last trumpet, for a trumpet will sound, and the dead will be raised incorruptible, and we shall all be changed."[35] What this is really saying is that Jesus, during his presence, will tell those that are the bride or church to "hold still" while he changes our DNA so that we are no longer sons of *Adam* but sons of *God*. At that time during his presence, he will present himself and all of his bride to the world of mankind! That's great news because the world of mankind can see the *means* of their salvation! Now let's consider verses 16–17: "because the Lord himself shall come down from heaven with a commanding shout by an archangel's voice and with God's trumpets, and the dead in Christ will rise again first, then we who remain alive be caught up together with them in the clouds to a meeting with the Lord in the air. And so we will always be with the Lord." Notice "caught up in the clouds"; this translation says "in the cloud" but "the" has been added. It is not in the Bible, so it really says "in clouds."[36]

To help everyone understand, I recommend reading the following verses in Ezekiel 38:15–16: "and you shall come from your place out of the recesses of the North, you and many people with you, all of them riding on horses, a great assembly, a mighty army. And you shall come up on my people Israel like a cloud, to cover the land, it shall be in the after days and I will bring you against my land, so that the nations may know me when I shall be sanctified in you before their eyes, O God!"[37] As you can see, an army is invading the nation of Israel, and it's like a large cloud or group of fighters coming in over the land. So Jesus will be gathering alive members of the bride in clouds or groups to meet the Lord in the air. To understand "meeting the Lord in the air," read Ephesians 2:2: "in which you then walked according to the course of this world, according to the ruler of the authority of the air, the spirit now working in the sons of disobedience." That spirit is Satan.[38]

John 8:44 says, "You are of the Devil as father and the lusts of your father you desire to do that one was a murderer from the beginning, and he has not stood in the truth because there is no truth in him when he speaks a lie, he the father of it."[39] So Satan is the ruler of the authority of the air over this world. This is part of the good news about the kingdom: while Satan is the spirit, now the ruler of the authority of the air, in the near future when Jesus arrives to a presence, he will present himself and the bride or a government that will take the place of Satan as ruler of the authority of the air. So the authority of the air will be Christ Jesus and his bride, Jesus will be the mediator between God and mankind, and the bride or the government to nurture mankind. This is described in Revelation 20:4–6: "and I saw thrones, and they sat on them, and judgment was given to them, and the souls of the ones having been beheaded because of the witness of Jesus, and because of the word of God, and who had not received the mark on their forehead and on their hand, and they lived and resigned with Christ a thousand years. But the rest of the dead did not live again until the thousand years were ended. This is the first resurrection, blessed and holy is the one having part in the first resurrection, the second death has no authority over these, but they will be priests of God and of Christ, and will reign with him a thousand years."₄₀ Notice this is the first resurrection, as Paul says in Philippians 3:11–12, "if somehow I may attain to the resurrection from the dead, not that I already received, or already have been perfected, but I press on, if I also may lay hold, in as much as I also was laid hold of by Christ Jesus."₄₁ Paul laid hold of this hope, which is to be a part of the bride of Christ, which is 144,000 in number, but unless God calls them to Christ, John 6:44 says, "no one is able to come to me unless the Father who sent me draws him, and I will raise him up in the last day."₄₂ So one does not decide that he or she is a part of the bride of Christ; Jehovah is the one that calls. Remember that Paul had been called, but Revelation 2:10 says, "Be faithful until death, and I will give you the crown of life."₄₃ So Paul wanted to be part of that resurrection referred to in Philippians 3:11 that he wanted to attain, and in the Greek it says, "out resurrection," meaning out of the resurrection of the world of mankind,₄₄ which Revelation 20:5 says is the first resurrection.₄₅ Next, Revelation 20:7–10 says, "And whenever the thousand years are ended Satan will be set loose out of his prison, and he will go to mislead the nations in the four corners of the earth, Gog and Magog, to assemble them in war, whose number is as the sand of the sea. And they went up over the Breadth of the land and encircled the camp of the saints, and the beloved city, and fire from God came down out of heaven and burned them down. And the Devil misleading them was thrown into the lake of fire and brimstone, where the beast and the false prophet were. And they were tormented day and night forever and ever."₄₆

So Satan, at the end of the thousand years, goes forth to mislead mankind. When Jesus and his bride take over the earth, all of mankind that are living under the rule of Jesus will be taught righteousness, but a good number will not love righteousness, so when Satan is turned loose, he will have no trouble getting these people to fight the saints, and at that time God sends fire to destroy all of them. Now let's read Revelation 20:11–12: "and I saw a great white throne and the one sitting on it, from whose face the earth and the heaven fled, and a place was not found for them and I saw the dead, the small and the great, standing before God, and books were opened and another book was opened, which is the book of Life, and the dead were judged out of the things written in the books, according to their works." Notice it says "I saw the dead, the small and the great standing before God."₄₇ Thus, it is *after* the judgment they got eternal life.

These are the ones described in Revelation 7:9–17: "after Jesus arrival these coming through the great tribulation and washing their robes white in the blood of Jesus."[48] These are alive when Jesus takes over the earth and are still alive after the thousand-year reign of Christ, and when the books are opened at judgment time, their names are found in the Book of Life, so they never die at all. John 11:24–26 says, "Martha said to him, I know that he will rise again in the resurrection. In the last day Jesus said to her, 'I am the resurrection and the life, the one believing into me though he die, he shall live, and everyone living and believing into me shall never ever die. Do you believe this?'"[49] Now we understand these are the people that we read about in Revelation 20:11–12, and it says these are the dead standing before God all through the thousand years as "legally dead," but after the judgment, they were legally alive.[50] Now let's read Revelation 20:13–14: "and the sea gave up the dead in it and death and Hades gave up the dead in them." They were each judged according to their works. Death and Hades were thrown into the lake of fire.[51]

When it says the sea (nations) gave up the dead in them, it is speaking of the second or general resurrection. You have to remember that all the other things God had accomplished, including the resurrection of the bride, or government of Christ Jesus, *was to make life available to mankind*! It is described in Revelation 21–22.[52] So Revelation 20:11–12 is speaking about those who are alive when Jesus and the bride take over the earth. They are dead legally but live through the thousand-year reign of Christ and have washed their robes white in the[53] blood of Christ. If you remember, these are the ones who never die at all. Revelation 20:13–15 speaks of those who are resurrected after the thousand-year reign of Christ; this is the second resurrection.[54] Revelation 21:1–4, in the start of that period of time, says, "And I saw a new heaven and a new earth, for the first heaven and the first earth passed away, and the sea no longer is (the sea is sinful mankind)," and Revelation 21:2–3 says, "I saw the Holy City, new Jerusalem, coming down out of heaven from God having been prepared as a Bride, having been adorned for her husband. I heard a great voice out of heaven say, behold, the tabernacle of God with men and he will tabernacle with them, and they will be his people and God himself will be with them as their God. God will wipe away every tear from their eyes and death shall be no longer. Nor mourning, nor outcry, nor pain will be any longer, for the first things passed away."[55]

So we have found out that the Tribulation started back in 325 AD, when the church became apostate, and as Matthew 24:22 says, "And except those days had been shortened, not any flesh would be saved."[56]

But Christ Jesus arrives in his presence or parousia in which he resurrects the dead in Christ and gathers those who are alive, presents himself and the bride to mankind, and destroys those who are threatening mankind. First Thessalonians 4:14–18 speaks of the same time.[57] First Thessalonians 4:15 speaks of his coming, which we found out that it is not coming, but presence; during the time of his resurrecting the dead, Christ gathers them together in clouds or groups and presents himself and his bride to the world of mankind.[58] So we can *see that the Rapture is impossible*! We found out that this is the first resurrection and that the second resurrection begins after the thousand-year reign of Christ and the old heaven and earth have passed away. So there is now the new heaven and new earth, which is the New Jerusalem coming from God, and then the resurrection of the world of mankind. This, dear friends, is the purpose of Jehovah which he *purposed before the founding of the world*. When you read John 3:16, it says, "For God so loved the world that he gave his only born son, that everyone believing into him should not parish, but have everlasting life."[59] Praise Jah you people.

Chapter 7

What the Seventh Chapter of Daniel Points To

I hope to show the events from the fourth beast of the seventh chapter of Daniel to the return of Jesus Christ.

From the fourth beast, there are three coverages to the return of Jesus Christ. By putting them together, we get the sequences which set the regular order of the events to Jesus Christ.

The first coverage: Daniel 7:7–14

It states: "And after this I looked in the night visions. And, behold, the fourth beast, fearful and terrifying, and very strong! And it had great iron teeth. It devoured and crushed, and stomped what was left with its feet. And it was different from all the beasts that were before it; and it had ten horns. I was thinking about the horns; and behold, another little horn came up among them, before whom three of the first horns were pulled up by the roots. And, behold, in this horn were eyes like the eyes of the man, and a mouth speaking great things.

"I was looking until the thrones were set up, and the Ancient of Days sat, whose robe was white as snow, and the hair of his head like pure wool. His throne was like flames of fire; its wheels like burning fire. A stream of fire went out and came out from before him. A thousand thousands served him, and a myriad myriads stood before him. The court was set, and the books were opened. Then I was looking because of the voice of the great words which the horn spoke. I was looking until the beast was killed, and his body was destroyed, and given to the burning flame.

"And the rest of the beasts, their dominion was taken away. Yet length of life was given them for a time and a season. I was looking in the night visions. And behold, one like the son of man came to the Ancient of Day. And they brought him near before Him. And dominion was given to Him, and glory, and a kingdom that all peoples, nations, and languages should serve Him. His dominion is an everlasting dominion which shall not pass away, and his kingdom that which shall not be destroyed.",[1] This is the first coverage, so let's review it to see what we can learn from it.

We know from history that the fourth beast is Rome, the sixth world power. The ten horns are Roman territory. I think they are Romania, Switzerland, Turkey, Poland, Austria, Croatia, Serbia, Bulgaria, Yugoslavia, and Hungary. Then another horn came up after the ten horns and pulled up by the roots three of those horns. They are Poland, Serbia, and Austria. The book *Hitler's Pope* by John Cornwell tells us who they are.[2]

Next, the Ancient of Days takes notice. His throne was a flame of fire, and a thousand thousands served him, and a myriad myriads stood before him. Books were opened, and the horn that came up after the ten horns was speaking great words. That horn is called a beast and was killed; his body was destroyed with burning fire!

Jehovah, the Ancient of Days, is the one that caused that horn and beast to be destroyed. Then the rest of the beasts had their dominions taken away, yet length of life was given them for a time and a season. Next, one like the son of man came to the Ancient of Days, and they brought him near before him. And dominion was given to him, and glory and a kingdom where all people, nations, and languages should serve him, and that kingdom would last forever.

I won't name the horn that was destroyed now, but I will later. But after the Ancient of Days destroyed that horn, he took away the dominion of all the beasts but extended their life for a season and a time. That is because he gave dominion to the kingdom of God, and the king of that kingdom is the son of man. So those beasts will exist for a while during the rule of the son of God.

The next coverage: Daniel 7:16–18

It states, "And I came near one of those who stood by and asked him the truth of all this. And he told me, and made me know the meaning of the things. These great beasts are four; they are four kings; they shall rise up out of the earth. But the saints of the Most High shall receive the kingdom and possess the kingdom forever, even forever and ever."[3]

This coverage tells us that there are four beasts and that they are kings, and the saints shall possess the kingdom forever, and forever and ever.

So now we know these beasts are kings.

The next coverage: Daniel 7:19-22

It states, "then I wanted to know the truth of the fourth beast, which was different from all of them, very frightening, whose teeth were of iron and its nails bronze; who devoured and crushed, and trampled what was left with its feet. And of the ten horns that were on its head, and the other which came up, and before whom three fell; even that horn that had eyes, and a mouth speaking great things, and its look was greater than his followers; I watched, and that horn made war with the saints and overcame them, until the Ancient of Days came, and judgment was given to the saints of the Most High; and the time came that the saints possessed the kingdom."[4]

This fourth beast was heartless and devoured anything standing against it. The horn coming up after the ten had eyes and a mouth that could see conditions around it and was speaking great things, and it was against the saints. And it made war against them and overcame them until it was time for the saints to possess the kingdom. We find out that there is a time for the kingdom to come.

The next coverage: Daniel 7:23-27

It states, "And he said, the fourth beast shall be the fourth kingdom on earth, which shall be different from all kingdoms, and shall devour all the earth and shall trample it down and crush it. And the ten horns out of this kingdom are ten kings; they shall rise; and another shall rise after them, and he shall be different from the first, and he shall humble three kings. And he shall speak words against the Most High, and shall wear out the saints of the Most High. And he intends to change times and law. And they shall be given into his hand until a time, and times and one-half time. But the judgment shall sit, and they shall take away his rulership, to cut off and to destroy until the end."[5]

This coverage adds some thoughts to the picture we now have of the ten horns and the other horn that comes up after the ten. The ten horns are really kings, and the horn that comes up later and wars with the saints and wears them out intends to change times and law.

Revelation 18:7-8 states, "By what things she glorified herself, and luxuriated, by so much give back to her torment and mourning's. Because she says in her heart, I sit as a queen, and I am not a widow: and I do not see mourning at all. Because of this, in one day her plagues shall come; death, and mourning, and famine; and she will be consumed with fire, for the Lord God judging her is strong."₆

So this horn is trying to change times and law, changing times by rejecting times of the horn's destruction. The word "law," according to *Merriam-Webster's Dictionary*, means "a rule of action established by authority."₇ The authority is Jehovah himself, and the horn wanted to change the law. And then it says the saints were given into the hand of the horn for a time, and time and one-half time. So this means that the horn that came up later will make war with the saints for quite some time. But how long a time is three and one-half times?

To help us, let's discuss the two witnesses dressed in sackcloth in Revelation 11:3–5. It says, "And I will give to my two witnesses, and they will prophecy a thousand two hundred and sixty days, dressed in sackcloth. Those are two olives trees, and the two lamp stands, standing before the God of the earth."₈ I think the fatness coming from the roots of the olive tree is the favor of God. One of these prophets is under the Law Covenant; the other prophet is under new covenant which God is writing in his mind, and heart, through the blood of Jesus Christ.

Now back to the two witnesses dressed in sackcloth, for 1,260 days. Numbers 14:34 says, "By the number of the days that you spied out the land, forty days, a day for each year, you answer for your errors forty years, as you must know what my being estranged means."₉ So we now have 1,260 years. I think the 1,260 years started in 935 BC. I refer you to the book *The Biblical Times* by Derek Williams. Page 126, under the subheading "Jerusalem," tells about King Solomon's seven hundred wives and three hundred concubines from many nations. These women all worshiped false gods and in some cases offered their baby as a sacrifice. I think you can see this would cause the prophet to prophesy in sackcloth.₁₀

So if you start at 935 BC and go forward 1,260 years, you come to 325 AD. That's when Constantine invited 250 bishops to Nicaea for a conference and the church became apostate and harlot by becoming the state religion; this was the abomination of desolation spoken of by Daniel the prophet in Daniel 11:30–32 and Matthew 24:15–22: "For the ships of Chittim will come against him. And he shall be grieved, and turn back, and be furious against the holy covenant, and he shall act. and will reform, and will heed those forsaking the holy covenant. And forces will stand from him, and they will profane the sanctuary, the fortress. And they shall remove the regular sacrifice; and they will place the desolating abomination."₁₁

This is the prophecy of Daniel that Matthew 24:15–22 is talking about. It says, "Therefore when you see the abomination of desolation, which was spoken of by Daniel the prophet, standing in the holy place – let those in Judea flee to the mountains; the one on the house top, let him not come down to take anything out of the house; and the one in the field, let him not turn back to take his garments. But pray that your flight will not be in winter, nor on a Sabbath. For there will be great affliction such as has not happened from the beginning of the world until now; no, nor ever will be. And except those days had been shortened, not any flesh would be saved."[12]

In Daniel 11:30, when it says, "And he shall act, and will return, and will heed those forsaking the holy covenant," this is Constantine. But where it says, "And they will profane the sanctuary," this is Constantine and the Catholic Church.[13]

Now back to the saints being given into the hands of the horns for three and one-half times. Here is my understanding: Three and one-half months equals 1,260 days, and when you apply one year for a day, you have 1,260 years. So the saints will be given into the hand of the horn that came up after the ten horns for 1,260 years.

So let's find out who that horn is. We just reviewed the conference at Nicaea in the year 325, when the church became apostate, after the second week they were locked out. The sons of God who did not accept the Father and the Son being equal began the Trinity. The rest became apostate and a harlot by becoming the state religion of Rome, that's the harlot referenced in Revelation 17:4–5, and it says she is the mother of the harlots, which is the Protestant religions. The mother of the harlots is the universal or the Catholic Church, and Protestant religions are all called Christendom. But the horn is the Catholic Church, and the Protestant religions are her children and will suffer the same fate.[14]

To further help us identify the Catholic Church as that horn, we now start with Daniel 11:33–35, which states, "And he will ruin by flatteries those who do evil against the covenant, but the people who know their God will be strong and will work, and those who understand among the people will teach many; yet they will stumble by the sword and the flame; by exile and spoil, for days. And when they stumble, they shall be helped with a little help, but many will join them with hypocrisy. And many of those who understand shall stumble, to refine and to purge them, and to make white, to the time of the end for it is yet for the appointed time." This is a very interesting part of Daniel's prophesy, which says, "And he will ruin by flatteries, those who do evil against the covenant.",₁₅ This is right after 325 AD when the sons of God fled to the mountains and small groups met to encourage each other. But the apostates were being flattered by Constantine and the Catholic Church. Then those bad forces came after the sons of God, with the sword and fire. The Bible says they had little help.

To help us understand, remember God had given the sons of God into the hand of that horn which is the apostate church, so God let his spirit be with them to help them endure and be faithful. That's why there has been no "groups of sons" sense that early time. That's why Matthew 24:21 says, "For there will be great affliction or tribulation, such as has not happened from the beginning of the world until now, no, nor ever will be.",₁₆ That started in 325 AD when the apostate church started, and they have fought against God since that time. That means they fight God's sons. God gave his sons into their hands until the end of this system of things. Now, I would like to quote from the first coverage in Daniel 7:9–14, which says, "I was looking until the thrones were set up, and the Ancient of Days sat, whose robe was white as snow, and the hair of his head like pure wool. His throne was like flames of fire; its wheels like burning fire. A stream of fire went out and came out from before him. A thousand thousands served him, and a myriad myriads stood before him, the court was set. and the books were opened. Then I was looking because of the voice of the great words which the horn spoke. I was looking until the beast was killed, and his body was destroyed, and given to the burning flames and the rest of the beasts had their dominion taken away. Yet length of life was given to them for a season and a time. I was in the night visions. And behold, one like the son of man came with the clouds of the heavens. And came he to the Ancient of Days. And they brought him near before him, and the dominion was given to him, and glory, and a kingdom, that all peoples, nations, and languages should serve him. His dominion is an everlasting dominion which shall not pass away, and his kingdom that which shall not be destroyed.",₁₇

What we learn here from this is that horn is also a beast, and the books were opened, and this beast is given to the burning flames, and his body is destroyed. This is the Catholic and Protestant churches; the Ancient of Days repaid them for how they treated God's sons. Notice the rest of the beasts had their dominion taken away, but length of life for a season and a time was given to them, and then dominion, and kingdom was given to the son of man, or Christ Jesus.

What this is showing is the Ancient of Days took action as described in Revelation 17:16–18. It says, "And the ten horns which you saw on the beast, these will hate the harlot, and will make her desolated and naked. And they will eat her flesh and will burn her down with fire. For God gave into their hearts to do his mind, and to give their kingdom to the beast, until the words of God shall be fulfilled. And this woman whom you saw is the great city; having a kingdom over the kings of the earth."[18]

So the Ancient of Days or Jehovah put it in their hearts to do away with this great harlot who has made the nations drunk with the wine of her fornication with the kings of the earth. And all those beasts or nations that had their dominion taken away are given life for a season and a time into the kingdom of Christ Jesus during the thousand-year rule. What this is saying is that people live in a nation, and the name of that nation will last for a time, and then the memory of those nations will fade away. So we know that Christendom will be destroyed, which will end the Great Tribulation that started in 325 AD. Then will come the kingdom of Christ Jesus, starting with the thousand-year rule. After the thousand-year rule of Jesus, the wild beast and the false prophet will be destroyed.

Before dealing with the wild beast and the false prophet, let's find out about the three and one-half times start that Daniel 7:25 talks about. It says, "And he will speak even words against the Most High, and he will harass continually the holy ones themselves of the supreme one, and he will intend to change times and law, and they will be given into his hand for a time and times and half a time."[19]

Let's compare Revelation 13:1, 3, 5–7. Verse 1 says, "And I saw a beast coming up out of the sea, having seven heads and ten horns, and on his horns ten diadems, and on its heads names of blasphemy."

Verse 3: "And I saw one of its heads, as having been slain to death, and its deadly wound was healed. And all the earth marveled after beast."

Verses 5–7: "And smooth speaking great things was given to it, and blasphemies. And authority to act forty-two months was given to it. And it opened its mouth in blasphemy toward God to blaspheme His name and his tabernacle, and those tabernacles in heaven. And it was given to it to war with the saints and to overcome them. And authority was given to it over every tribe and tongue and nation."[20] In Daniel 7:25, the horn (Catholic Church) is speaking against the Most High and the holy ones and given into his hands three and one-half times.[21]

Revelation 13:1, 3, 5–7 talk about the same thing, but verse 3 speaks about the beast that was slain to death and brought back to life. This is about Rome. Revelation 13:5 states, "A mouth speaking great things given to it, and blasphemies, and authority to act forty-two months was given to it." That mouth is the horn, or the Catholic Church, and the saints are given into her hands for forty-two months. And the woman (Catholic Church) riding on this beast which you saw was and is not and is about to come up out of the abyss and goes to perdition. A few lines down, it states the beast was a thing, and is not, yet now is. What this seems to say is that Rome went into the abyss in the year 476 AD, and the time it comes out of the abyss is when the forty-two months, time, times and one-half time, or three and one-half times start. What we have seen is 1,260 years, so when was Rome coming up out of the abyss? This information that I am giving is found in the Wikipedia encyclopedia found on the Internet.[22] Charlemagne became the king of the Frankish Empire in the year 768 AD, but the Holy Roman Empire did not come until 800 AD. When the pope anointed Charlemagne as king of Rome, he made him emperor of the Franks and Rome. Since Revelation chapter 17 states the beast (Holy Roman Empire) was coming up out of the abyss, the best date I can give is 768 AD. If you go forward 1,260 years from 768, you have 2028 AD. I have already said I am not sure of this date, but I do think that it is close to that date. Now Daniel in 7:11–12 states, "Then I was looking because of the voice words which the horn spoke. I was looking until the beast was killed and his body was destroyed and given to the burning flame. And the rest of the beasts, their dominion was taken away. Yet length of life was given them for a time and a season."[23] And then it shows the son of man coming to the Ancient of Days and is given the kingdom forever and forever. So just before 2028 or about, that horn we now know as the Catholic Church and Protestant churches will be destroyed.

While the Catholic and the Protestant organizations will be destroyed, the people who belong to these organizations, if they accept the blood of Jesus's sacrifice, will get eternal life. Jehovah loved the world of mankind before the world was created. So you as a part of the world of mankind needs to know that Jehovah loves you and knows you. Jehovah knows you are sinners and fall short of the glory of Jehovah, but because he sees good in you and me, and through the sacrifice of his son, Jesus, he has bought all of us—that's you and me!

And now, let's turn our attention to the two-horned beast. Revelation 13:12–18 states, "And I saw another beast coming up out of the earth. And it had two horns like a lamb, but spoke like a dragon.

And it executes all the authority of the first beast before it. And it causes that the earth and those dwellings in it should worship the first beast, of which were healed its deadly wound. And it does great signs that even fire it causes to come down out of the heaven onto the earth before men. And it deceives those dwelling on the earth because of the signs which were given to it to do before the beast saying to those dwelling on the earth to make an image of the beast who has the wound of the sword and lived. And was given to it to give a spirit to the image, of the beast, so that the image of the beast might even speak, and might cause as many as would not worship the image of the beast to be killed. And the small and the great, and the rich and the poor, and the free men and the slaves, it causes that they give to them all a mark on their right hand or on their foreheads, even that not any could buy or sell, except those having the mark or the name of the beast, or the number of its name. Here is wisdom: let him having reason count the number of the beast, for it is the number of a man- and its number is six hundred and sixty-six."[24]

So the two-horned beast tells the people of the earth to make an image of the beast that went into the abyss and came back to life. The United Nations has to be the image, for the seven world powers and the ten horns all belong to it. And while it was supposed to bring peace to the earth, there are small wars all around the earth. The United Nations holds talks between enemies, although it does not seem to do much good. But looking at the world scene, it looks like we are heading to a third world war, this time with nuclear weapons.

In the thirteenth chapter of Revelation, the two-horned lamb takes action. Verses 15–17 states, "And he was then given to it to give a spirit to the image of the beast, so that the image of the beast might even speak, and might cause as many as would not worship the image of the beast to be killed. And the small and the great, and the rich and the poor, and the free man and the slaves, it cause that they give to them all a mark on their right hand, or on their foreheads even that not any could buy or sell, except those having the mark, or the name of the beast or the number of its name." What this is saying is that the nation, or two-horned lamblike beast, gives spirit or money to the image so that it can get a mark on the right hand or forehead, that those on earth who take in knowledge (forehead) or support (right hand) those who don't worship the image to be killed, and those who reject the mark could not buy or sell.[25]

Revelation 19:20 states, "And the beast was seized, and with this one the false prophet doing signs before it, by which he deceived those having received the mark of the beast, and those worshiping its image."[26] So the two-horned lamblike beast is a false prophet. So those not worshiping the image are not killed, or those not having the mark on their right hand or forehead continue to buy and sell. The reason is the United Nations has no power! And the two-horned lamblike beast is a false prophet.

Now, we want to see who this two-horned beast that becomes a false prophet is. That two-horned lamb that became a false prophet is the United States. Only this nation has caused fire to come down out of the heave and space exploration, when man walked on the moon, and other great works; it says it deceived those dwelling on the earth.

I would like to say something about that in Revelation 12:9. It says that Satan deceived the whole world, that he is evil, because Satan knew better. But I don't think the United States knew better. I think it believed what it was doing was right. Even so, the world was deceived. The United Nations has not and will not bring peace to the nations.[27]

More on the United States: Most people today think that the United States was founded by Christians; nothing could be further from the truth. The people who founded the United States were mostly Masons, according to *The Goddess, The Grail and The Lodge,* a book by Alan Butler. I want to share parts of it with you regarding what the Masons did in behalf of the nation's beginning.

I will be quoting from pages 304–310: "The capitol was designed to be the legislative and democratic seat of the United States of America. Initially conceived, as was the original conception of the entire city, by Pierre Charles L'Enfant, the capitol stands at the elevated east end of the mall. The site was, in L'Enfant's words, 'a pedestal waiting for a monument.' The architect who finally won approval for his design for the capitol itself was Dr. William Thornton, a man of Scottish extract and a noted Freemason. It is suggested that the floor plan of the capitol mall was based upon that of a Masonic temple- an east-west rectangle, attached to an unfinished triangle. In a lodge, the Grand Master would preside at the point of the triangle, which is precisely where the capitol stands on the mall. In essence, the capitol is little more than a deliberately engineered temple and stands as an integral part of a street plan which is, itself, living proof of the knowledge of sacred architecture possessed by those who meticulously planned the city. Like so many buildings in Washington, the most telling aspect of the capitol's true spiritual heritage lays in the state of the heavens at the time the corner stone was laid. In the case of the capitol, this ceremony took place on the 16th of September 1793. The corner stone ceremony took place after a solemn and dignified procession, in which a number of Masonic lodges took conspicuous part. At their head, and wearing full Masonic regalia, was George Washington himself. The stone was almost certainly laid at midday. It is relatively simple to draw up an astrological chart for an event such as this and we can be in no doubt that to the astrologically minded Freemasons, who had organized and planned the event, an auspicious chart of the heavens would be deemed necessary before the stone laying would have been arranged. In many circles astrology was still accepted as not just important, but crucial, at the end of the eighteenth century. We are most familiar these days with personal astrology. The position of the stars and planets at the time of one's birth is said to set the seed on the sort of character a child will grow to enjoy, and is also said to play an important part in life events thereafter.

"Astrologers at the time of the founding of the United States of America believed whole heartedly that any enterprise, or building, also responded to the positive and negative attributes of the time at which it was instigated. And astrologer would therefore seek the most providential planetary positions and aspects for something as important as the commencement of a building such as the capitol. The time chosen is most telling. At noon on the 18th of September 1783, the sign of the zodiac that was immediately overhead, and therefore, astrologically the most potent, was Virgo. The sun, which from an astrological perspective, would have to smile on such an event, was at 26 degrees of Virgo. In fact the mid heaven and the sun were within four minutes of occupying the same position in the sky, so it is possible the cornerstone ceremony actually took place at four minutes before noon, when mid heaven and sun would have been together, or in astrological terms, conjunct.

"To any astrologer this is very telling. The capitol building was so pivotal to the embryonic United States that it deserved the best possible 'birth.' Virgo, as we have seen, is indisputably the zodiac sign most sacred to Goddess worshipers. It is the sign of the Virgin. Close to the end of the zodiac sign is the Constellation of Crator, and the sun on that day in Washington was in direct contact with this most potent symbol of Goddess adoration.

"Those planning the ceremony could have chosen any day, or any time within any day to perform the necessary rites. However, they made it absolutely plain that the very azimuth of their devotions was Virgo, and with it the first goddess, the "Providence" of George Washington and patroness and founding spirit of the new utopia. The capitol is certainly a temple, and it is one deliberately built to venerate the Goddess. It was inspired by Freemasonic and Rosicrucian knowledge and was as much a legacy of the golden thread as any of the Gothic cathedrals of Europe."

I noticed this book gave two dates for the laying of the cornerstone; one has to be wrong. I think the right one is September 18, 1783, which is seven years after 1776, the founding of the United States. It sounds reasonable that the planning and laying of the cornerstone would be seven years later. I am sure you have noticed that the Masons who founded the United States worshipped goddesses and regarded all the planets as goddesses.

For example, the planet called Earth is called Mother Earth, and all the planets are female; put them together and you have the Great Goddess of the Universe. In other words, they look to the universe for direction. To show that it was not Christendom, we will quote from a few of them.

Thomas Jefferson, the one who penned the American Constitution and later became president of the United States stated, "I have examined all the known superstitions of the world, and I do not find in our particular superstition of Christianity one redeeming feature. … Millions of innocent men, women and children, since the introduction of Christianity have been burnt, tortured, fined, and imprisoned. What has been the effect of this coercion? To make one half of the world gods and the other half hypocrites; is to support roguery and error all over the earth."

John Adams: "The doctrine of the divinity of focus is made a convenient lover for absurdity." Adams made his views regarding the spiritual nature of the government of the United States abundantly clear when he signed the Treaty of Tripoli. He supervised the construction of the document himself, and article II states, "The government of the United States is by no means founded on the Christian religion."

James Madison, the fourth president of the United States: "What influence in fact have Christian ecclesiastical establishments had on civil society? In many instances they have been upholding the thrones of political tyranny. In no instance have they been seen as the guardians of the liberties of the people. Rulers who wished to subvert the public liberty have found in the clergy convenient auxiliaries. A just government, instituted to secure and perpetuate liberty, does not need the clergy."[28]

We all know the history of Adam and Eve. Eve was deceived into thinking that God was wrong and that she could establish her own standard of right and wrong. Adam knew better but accepted her standard and disobeyed God. This was the beginning of man's rule, and it caused death to the human family. And we found out that the founders of the United States looked at how the planets were lined up, and man made his decision on material things, and that's why the United States became a false prophet.

Now let's review Revelation 13:18, which states, "Here is wisdom: let him having reason count the number of the beast, for it is the number of a man- and its number is six hundred and sixty-six." But if you look at the Greek verse, it states "the number of man," not "a man."[29] Take $600 \times 10 = 6{,}000$; take $60 \times 100 = 6{,}000$; take $six \times 1{,}000 = 6{,}000$. I think man has been on the earth almost six thousand years. I think the kingdom of God will start in a few years, and then Christ Jesus will start a one-thousand-year rule which will make a seven-thousand-year day. You see in Genesis 1:1 that "In the beginning God created the heavens and the earth." Most people think that the age of the earth is four million to seven million years, but the Bible says after God created the heavens and the earth, the earth was covered with water and in darkness. Then there was six 7,000-year days preparing the earth and creating animals, marine life, and man and woman at the end of the sixth day. And we are almost through six thousand years of the seventh day. Six thousand years of man's rule and Jesus will soon begin a one-thousand-year rule. But that rule will be different—it will be God's rule. You see the kingdom will be God's, and he gave the son of God, Jesus, dominion to rule with God's standard, which the first Adam rejected, but the second Adam, Jesus, will be obedient to his father, Jehovah, and that will be the beginning of God's divine purpose started before the creation of mankind.

God knew the first Adam would bring death on all his sons and daughters. Since that time, God loved you and me. Now I know some of you have a low opinion of yourselves, and all of us are sinners, but God sees the heart of all of us and when you do kind acts for someone, God sees value or potential in you, and that's why God loves you. You are valuable to him, and he has a bright future for you. That is God's divine purpose. So when you see Christendom destroyed, you who were a slave to those religions are now free at last in Christ Jesus, in the kingdom of Jehovah. So look at Revelation chapter 18: "And I heard another voice out of heaven saying my people, come out of her, that you may not share in her sins. And that you may not receive of her plagues." To most of mankind, your future is bright!

From the Author

I have just finished writing this book, *The Coming Seismic Eruption of Christendom*. I think I have been preparing to write this book since I was fourteen years old.

I grew up on a farm and we as a family attended a Baptist church. I remember the people who attended that church being very kind and generous. The pastor talked about being saved, which to my understanding was at death, the soul of that person went to heaven to be with Jesus. Those who were not saved at death went to hell for eternity. The earth was eventually to be burned up. This meant that those souls who went to hell would be tormented forever. The pastor also referred to God and Jesus as being the same, which was confusing and unsettling to me.

There was a highway that ran through our farm property and a small stream of water that flowed through a culvert under the highway. One day I was lying on the culvert, and the thought came to mind that I would like to try to talk to whoever was in charge of everything. As presumptuous as it sounds, that is the way I started my prayer, saying I want to talk to whoever is in charge. If through Jesus, fine, but if not, no offense, I just want to talk to whoever is in charge. I just wanted to know what the future was for the earth and for mankind, for the thought of going to heaven did not appeal to me at all. These thoughts would reappear from time to time.

After World War II and my service in the Merchant Marines, I was now twenty-one years old. My good friend and cousin went to Half Moon Lake. My friend had a cabin there. My cousin, whose name was Willard, had bought a new outboard motor, so he and my friend put it on a boat at the cabin and took it out fishing for a while. Then Willard and I went fishing. Then, as it was getting late, we started back, and at that time, the metal bottom of the boat came loose, and the boat sank. We sighted what we thought was the nearest land and started swimming in that direction. Willard had been in the navy and on the Navy Swim Team, so I was not worried about him, but I knew I could not make it to land. I was heavy in the water and not a good swimmer. After we were about a third distance to land, Willard said he could not go further. He could float but would not try. I thought he was going to drown, but I could not leave him. As I started swimming over to him, he saw what I was doing and just went under the water. Knowing Willard, he did this to make me start swimming again for land. I was soon down to a dog paddle. So at twenty-one years of age, I approached whoever was in charge and explained to him I was about to die and did not know about the future of the earth and what was the future for mankind. I did not understand why I was born; at that time the thought came to me about getting out of the lake. I told whoever was in charge that if he would help me, I was going to try to get to land. I finally made it to land, and the first thing I did was to tell whoever was in charge "Thank you" and that I was going to do my best to find out who he was and his purpose for mankind.

I then started walking toward what I thought was the direction of the cabin. I came across a fallen tree, continued walking, and climbed over another fallen tree the same size. The third time I recognized the same tree, so I decided I was dead and in purgatory, so I just sat down and gave up. About that same time, my friend from the cabin was driving my car with the spotlight shining trying to locate us, and I saw that I had ended on a small island and I then knew I was not dead or in purgatory, and they sent a small boat to rescue me.

After this experience, I started seriously trying to find out "whoever was in charge." I studied with the Watchtower people who called themselves "Jehovah's Witnesses" and learned some good things such as the earth will be here forever, that it is the home of mankind, the soul is you, and hell is not a place of eternal torment. Jesus is not part of a Trinity but is the son of God.

Now we get to what I think is wrong. They said that Jesus came invisibly first in the year 1884 and that the end of the world would come in that generation. That did not happen. Then they said that Jesus came in the year 1914 invisibly, and that generation would not pass away until the end of the world. That did not happen. They said that the bride of Christ or the church will be spirits in heaven and that Jesus is also a spirit, that he is not coming in the flesh. Acts 13:34–37 says, "And that He raised from the dead, no more about to return to corruption, so he has said, 'I will give you the holy things of faithful David,' also said in another, 'You will not give your Holy One to see corruption' for having served his own generation by the Counsel of God, David truly fell asleep and was added to his fathers, and saw corruption. But he whom God raised up, he did not see corruption." And 2 John 7 says, "Because many deceivers went out into the world, those not confessing Jesus Christ to have come in the flesh – this is the deceiver and the antichrist." This translation says "to have come," past tense, but in the Greek it says "Jesus Christ coming in the flesh." *Strong's Concordance* reference number is 2064, and that is future tense. Look at Matthew 24:30 where it refers to the "Son of Man coming on the clouds of heaven." You know that is future, and *Strong's* reference number is 2064 and says the same as 2 John 7.

In my opinion, the Watchtower organization is a part of the Antichrist group. I have been disassociated from that organization since April of 1987. There are many good and sincere people who are part of that group as with those of other religious organizations who may find they have been deceived also.

Since that time, 1987, I have been studying the Bible and doing additional research with regard to the question "whoever is in charge" asked when I was fourteen and again when I was twenty-one. I now know the "who" is Jehovah God, and he is in charge. I have learned that he is bigger than the universe, all energy comes from him, and he is the source of all life.

I have learned that Jesus, who was first known as the Word, was God's first creation (Revelation 3:14) and that later, as the Word, he created the universe, then mankind, animals, sea life, and the birds. After that, the Word became flesh, which made him the son of God, and we all need to let Jesus be the lord of our lives, and that gives us a standing with Jehovah, truly the God of love. Christendom has kept mankind from truly knowing Jesus as the son of God and from knowing Jehovah God and his love.

Endnotes

CHAPTER 1

1. *Strong's Concordance* reference number 1080.
2. Bible translation by Jay P. Green, Sr., John 3:3.
3. Ibid., Acts 13:3–34.
4. *Strong's Concordance* reference number 1080.
5. Bible translation by Jay P. Green, Sr., Matt. 1:1.
6. *Strong's Concordance* reference number 1080.
7. Bible translation by Jay P. Green, Sr., John 3:16.
8. Bible translation by James Moffatt, John 3:16.
9. *Strong's Concordance* reference number 3439.
10. Richard E. Rubenstein, *When Jesus Became God,* 76–223.
11. Bible translation by Jay P. Green, Sr., Luke 7:12.
12. Ibid., Col. 1:15.
13. Ibid., Rev. 3:14.
14. Ibid., John 1:14.
15. Ibid., Luke 1:35.
16. Ibid., Matt. 12:47.

CHAPTER 2

1. Bible translation by Jay P. Green, Sr., Matt. 24:24.
2. Ibid., Rev. 12:9.
3. Ibid., 1 John 2:18.
4. *Strong's Concordance* (Hebrew) reference number 7585; (Greek) reference number 86.

5. Paul Johnson, *A History of Christianity,* 289.
6. *King James Bible* translation of Ps. 49:15 and Ps. 55:15 with a margin.
7. Bible translation by Jay P. Green, Sr., Rev. 20:18.
8. *Strong's Concordance* reference number 1067.
9. Bible translation by Jay P. Green, Sr., Mark 9:48.
10. Ibid., Rev. 20:14.
11. Ibid., John 3:16.
12. Ibid., Heb. 10:26.
13. *Strong's Concordance* (Hebrew) reference number 5315.
14. Bible translation by Jay P. Green, Sr., Gen. 1:30.
15. Ibid., Gen. 2:14.
16. Ibid., Ezek. 18:4.
17. Ibid., John 3:16.
18. Ibid., Gen. 1:28.
19. Ibid., 2:17.
20. Ibid., 3:1–6.
21. Ibid., 1 Tim. 2:14.
22. Ibid., Col. 5:21–22.
23. Ibid., Gen. 3:22–24.
24. Ibid., Rev. 22:1–14.
25. The American Standard Bible translation, 2 Cor. 5:1.
26. Bible translation by Jay P. Green, Sr., 1 Cor. 3:9.
27. Ibid., Eph. 2:19–22.
28. Ibid., 1 Cor. 6:19.
29. Ibid., John 1:1–3.
30. Ibid., Rev. 3:14.
31. Ibid., Ps. 90:2.
32. Ibid., John 14:28.
33. Ibid., Heb. 1:8.
34. Ibid., 1 John 4:1–3.
35. Ibid., 2 John 1:7.
36. *Strong's Concordance* reference number 2014.
37. Bible translation by Jay P. Green, Sr., 1 John 4:1–3.
38. Ibid., Matt. 24:30.

CHAPTER 3
1. Bible translation by Jay P. Green, Sr., Isa. 9:6–7.
2. Ibid., Acts 2:29–32.
3. Ibid., 1 Pet. 3:18–19.
4. Ibid., Acts 2:31–32.

5. Ibid., 1 Tim. 2:5.
6. Ibid., 1 Pet. 3:18.
7. Ibid., Acts 7:59.
8. Ibid., Luke 23:42–43.
9. Ibid., 33:46.
10. Ibid., 1:46–47.
11. *Strong's Concordance* reference number 1722.
12. Ibid., reference number 3739.
13. Bible translation by Jay P. Green, Sr., 1 John 3:2.
14. Ibid., Acts 2:31.
15. Ibid., John 20:19–20.
16. Ibid., Isa. 9:6–7.
17. Ibid., Acts 24:15.
18. Ibid., 2 Cor. 3:18–22.

CHAPTER 4
1. Bible translation by Jay P. Green, Sr., chapters 12–22:5.
2. Ibid., Gen. 22:6–18.
3. Ibid., Heb. 11:1.
4. *Strong's Concordance* reference number 5287.
5. Bible translation by Jay P. Green, Sr., Gen. 17:11.
6. *Strong's Concordance* reference number 226.
7. Bible translation by Jay P. Green, Sr., Exod. 12:44.
8. Ibid., Gal. 5:3.
9. Ibid., 3:24.
10. Ibid., 3:16.
11. Ibid., John 3:16.
12. *Strong's Concordance* reference number 1080.
13. Bible translation by Jay P. Green, Sr., Rev. 3:14.
14. Ibid., Heb. 11:17.
15. *Strong's Concordance* reference number 3439.
16. Bible translation by Jay P. Green, Sr., Gen. 22:16.
17. *Strong's Concordance* reference number 3173.
18. Bible translation by Jay P. Green, Sr., Exod. 19:5–6.
19. Ibid., Matt. 25:37–39.
20. Ibid., Ps. 118:26.
21. Ibid., Rom. 2:28–29.
22. Ibid., 11:30–32.
23. Ibid., Exod. 19.
24. Ibid., Luke 12:32.

25. Ibid., Rev. 14:1–8.
26. Ibid., 1 Cor. 5:17.
27. Ibid., Rev. 14:7–8.
28. Ibid., Deut. 32:32–33.
29. Ibid., Rev. 3:14.
30. Ibid., 14:8.
31. Ibid., 7:1–4.
32. Ibid., Gal. 3:19.
33. Ibid., Heb. 8:10–13.
34. Ibid., Luke 12:32.
35. Ibid., John 6:44.
36. Ibid., Rom. 8:15–16.
37. Ibid., 6:3–11.
38. Ibid., John 3:3.
39. Ibid., 3:6–7.
40. Ibid., Rom. 8:8–11.
41. Ibid., 1 Cor. 15:51–53.
42. Ibid., Rev. 7:9–17.
43. Ibid., Isa. 6:1.
44. Ibid., Matt. 24:21–22.
45. Ibid., Rev. 17:6.
46. Ibid., Gen. 3–15.
47. Ibid., Rev. 12.
48. Ibid., Lev. 23.
49. Ibid., Acts 1:4–5.
50. Ibid., John 20:21–23.
51. Ibid., Acts 19:6.
52. Ibid., Rev. 12:1–2.
53. Ibid., Col. 1:12–13.
54. Ibid., Gal. 4:22–26.
55. Ibid., Heb. 12:22.

CHAPTER 5
1. Bible translation by Jay P. Green, Sr., Rev. 12:9.
2. Ibid., John 8:38–44.
3. Ibid., Mark 12:29–32.
4. *Strong's Concordance* reference number 1520.
5. Bible translation by Jay P. Green, Sr., John 1:1.
6. Ibid., Rev. 3:14.
7. *Strong's Concordance* reference number 848.

8. Bible translation by Jay P. Green, Sr., John 1:14.
9. Ibid., John 1:1–5.
10. Ibid., John 8.
11. Ibid., 1 Cor. 8:5–6.
12. Ibid., Ps. 90:2.
13. Ibid., John 3:16.
14. Ibid., Kings 8:27.
15. Ibid., Isa. 46:9–10.
16. Ibid., 1 Pet. 1:19–20.
17. Ibid., John 1:14.
18. Ibid., Matt. 28:19–20.
19. *Strong's Concordance* reference number 3686.
20. Bible translation by Jay P. Green, Sr., Judg. 15:14.
21. Ibid., Isa. 40:26.
22. Ibid., 1 John 4:16.
23. Ibid., Ps. 90:2.
24. Ibid., 1 Tim. 6:16.
25. Ibid., Ps. 83:18.
26. Ibid., Deut. 6:4.
27. Ibid., Mark 12:29–30.
28. Ibid., Gen. 17:1.
29. Ibid., Exod. 3:13–15.
30. *Strong's Concordance* reference number 1961.
31. Bible translation by Jay P. Green, Sr., Gen. 19:26.
32. Ibid., John 3:16.
33. Ibid., Matt. 6:9.

CHAPTER 6
1. *Strong's Concordance* reference numbers 386, 450, 1453, and 1080.
2. Bible translation by Jay P. Green, Sr., Acts 13:33.
3. Ibid., Ps. 2:7.
4. *Strong's Concordance* reference numbers 2227 and 5513.
5. Bible translation by Jay P. Green, Sr., Gen. 1:21–22.
6. Ibid., Ezek. 18:4.
7. Bible translation by Jay P. Green, Sr.
8. Ibid., John 3:16.
9. Tim Lahaye, *A Quick Look at the Rapture and the Second Coming*, 18–19.
10. Bible translation by Jay P. Green, Sr., Matt. 24:15–22.
11. Ibid., Luke 21:20–24.
12. Ibid., Dan. 11:29–32.

13. Ibid., 1 Pet. 2:4–5.
14. Richard E. Rubenstein, *When Jesus Became God*.
15. Jacob Burckhardt, *The Age of Constantine the Great*.
16. Ibid.
17. Bible translation by Jay P. Green, Sr., Dan. 11:28–32.
18. Rubenstein, *When Jesus Became God*, 76.
19. Bible translation by Jay P. Green, Sr., Matt. 24:15–16.
20. Ibid., Rom. 2:28–29.
21. *Strong's Concordance* reference number 2347.
22. Bible translation by Jay P. Green, Sr., Matt. 24:11–16.
23. Ibid., 24:21–22.
24. Ibid., 24:23–28.
25. *Strong's Concordance* reference number 3952.
26. Bible translation by Jay P. Green, Sr., Phil. 1:26, 2:12.
27. Ibid., Matt. 24:28.
28. Ibid., 24:29–31.
29. Ibid., Eph. 2.
30. Ibid., 1 Thess. 4:14–18.
31. *Strong's Concordance* reference number 5952.
32. Lahaye, *A Quick Look at the Rapture and the Second Coming*, 18.
33. Bible translation by Jay P. Green, Sr., 1 Thess. 4:16–17.
34. *Strong's Concordance* reference number 3952.
35. Bible translation by Jay P. Green, Sr., 1 Cor. 15:51–52.
36. Ibid., 1 Thess. 4:16–17.
37. Ibid., Ezek. 38:15–16.
38. Ibid., Eph. 2:2.
39. Ibid., John 8:44.
40. Ibid., Rev. 20:4–6.
41. Ibid., Phil. 3:11–12.
42. Ibid., John 6:44.
43. Ibid., Rev. 2:10.
44. Ibid., Phil. 3:11.
45. Ibid., Rev. 20:5.
46. Ibid., 20:7–10.
47. Ibid., 20:11–12.
48. Ibid., 7:9–17.
49. Ibid., John 11:24–26.
50. Ibid., Rev. 20:11–12.
51. Ibid., 20:13–14.
52. Ibid., chapters 21–22.

53. Ibid., Rev. 20:11–12.
54. Ibid., 20:13–15.
55. Ibid., 21:2–3.
56. Ibid., Matt. 24:22.
57. Ibid., 1 Thess. 4:14–18.
58. Ibid., 4:15.
59. Ibid., John 3:16.

CHAPTER 7
1. Bible translation by Jay P. Green, Sr., Dan. 7:7–14.
2. John Cornwall, *Hitler's Pope*, 48–51, 222–233, 250–257.
3. Bible translation by Jay P. Green, Sr., Dan. 7:16–18.
4. Ibid., 7:19–22.
5. Ibid., 7:23–27.
6. Ibid., Rev. 18:7–8.
7. *Merriam-Webster's Dictionary*, "law."
8. Bible translation by Jay P. Green, Sr., Rev. 11:3–5.
9. Ibid., Num. 14:34.
10. Derek Williams, *The Biblical Times*.
11. Bible translation by Jay P. Green, Sr., Dan. 11:30–32.
12. Ibid., Matt. 24:15–22.
13. Ibid., Dan. 11:30.
14. Ibid., Rev. 17:4–5.
15. Ibid., Dan. 11:33–35.
16. Ibid., Matt. 24:21.
17. Ibid., Dan. 7:9–14.
18. Ibid., Rev. 17:16–18.
19. Ibid., Dan. 7:25.
20. Ibid., Rev. 13:1, 3, 5–7.
21. Ibid., Dan. 7:25.
22. Wikipedia, "Internet."
23. Bible translation by Jay P. Green, Sr., Dan. 7:11–12.
24. Ibid., Rev. 13:12–18.
25. Ibid., 13:15–17.
26. Ibid., 19:20.
27. Ibid., 12:9.
28. Alan Butler, *The Goddess, the Grail and the Lodge*.
29. Bible translation by Jay P. Green, Sr., Rev. 13:18.

www.ingramcontent.com/pod-product-compliance
Lightning Source LLC
Chambersburg PA
CBHW060342080526
44584CB00013B/878